NILS P. HAUGEN

PIONEER AND POLITICAL REMINISCENCES

By

Nils P. Haugen

Reprinted from the *Wisconsin Magazine of History* Volumes XI, XII, and XIII

PUBLICATIONS
OF THE
STATE HISTORICAL SOCIETY

OF WISCONSIN

EDITED BY

JOSEPH SCHAFER

SUPERINTENDENT OF THE SOCIETY

THE ANTES PRESS, Evansville, Wisconsin, *State Printers*

PIONEER AND POLITICAL REMINISCENCES

CHAPTER I

GETTING A START IN WISCONSIN

The fact that my father, Peder N. Haugen, with his family came to Wisconsin in 1854 and became a pioneer settler in Pierce County the next year, has caused some friends to suggest that I write my recollections of our entry into the country and early experiences in the then unsettled section of the state. My active participation in the political life of the state from the seventies till recent times may have been an additional reason for the suggestion.

The causes that gave rise to emigration from Norway have been variously stated. The dissatisfaction with the dominance of the state church has often been given as one cause. In the case of my father, however, the main reason was the hope and expectation of bettering his economic condition. He had no quarrel with the church. He had taught parochial school during his youth for some ten years, thereby earning exemption from military service. His certificate of this exemption I have. Military service in Norway began at the age of twenty-two. I believe that is still the law. Father did have some objection to subjecting young men to this forced service each summer during the best years of their youth, which might be put to better advantage in some lucrative employment; and this may have been one motive in taking his three sons out of the country. On a visit to Norway in 1907 I suggested to some friends that it would seem more in harmony with the rule of other countries to fix the military service at an earlier age than twenty-two. The answer was that maturity was not reached as early in the northern countries as in the more southern and in America. I called attention to the fact that Scandinavian boys served in the Civil War when eighteen years old, and even younger, and kept pace with the native Americans, and that in the industries generally, including lumbering in forest and mill, they had not failed to do their share fully with others of the same age.

It was not a general objection to military service that actuated my father, but he thought that the situation in Norway furnished no call for keeping up the show of an army that took the young men out of the economic service during their best years. He was not misled by exaggerated stories of "getting rich quick," but he was strong and healthy, and mother was intelligently industrious and economical. The lure of better opportunities for the children resulted in their selling the little farm of some sixty acres and some of their personalty in the spring of 1854, and breaking away from friends and old associations. Immigration into the United States from Norway reached the high point that year. Besides being a farmer, father was a blacksmith, having acquired this vocation early in his father's shop. He was a handy craftsman with tools, not only in iron but in wood as well.

THE JOURNEY

There were no steamships with present-day luxuries sailing from Norway in 1854. We sailed from the city of Drammen. It must have been in the early part of April, for we reached Chicago on July 4 after spending nine weeks and two days on the ocean, besides more than a week in the journey from Quebec to Chicago. Being stowed away under deck on a sailing vessel with little or no ventilation, in fair and stormy weather, some two hundred and fifty passengers in one room practically, with rows of double bunks (*a la* Pullman sleeper), and with seasickness prevalent, was not particularly conducive to happiness and joviality; but youthful passengers no doubt found some means of enjoyment. The general route of the vessel lay to the north of Scotland, but a storm on the North Sea took us through the English Channel, where we saw the white cliffs of Dover, the estuary of the Thames, and the first steam vessels. On the Banks of Newfoundland we encountered the usual icebergs. On the whole the passage was normal for the times. Two deaths occurred, a man and a child; both were buried at sea, the captain officiating. We had a view of the Falls of Montmorency and cast anchor in the port of Quebec, where farewells were taken with the genial captain and we were left on the shore to continue our journey by steamboat to Montreal. A little occurrence took place as the Norwegian immigrants were entering the steerage of the boat. A couple of deck hands got into a scrap resulting in bloody noses, which made one of our fellow passengers, an old woman, remark: "Oh, the devil seems to be here too!" And it seemed to be the same old devil she thought she had left behind in Norway.

At Montreal change was again made and we had our first railroad experience. Another change seems to have been made before we reached Buffalo, for we saw Niagara Falls from the American side. Father told us they were "the largest waterfalls in the world." I do not claim to have the wonderful memory of Anatole France's "Petit Pierre," but unusual events like breaking up a childhood home and the trip on ocean and land would in all probability impress themselves on the memory of any normal five-year-old child.

Thirty-five years later I saw Niagara again, and knew at once that it was the American falls I had seen as a child, and not the "Horse Shoe."

We took boat at Buffalo for Detroit. And it was on Lake Erie that the saddest part of our journey commenced. Cholera broke out among the immigrants, and many deaths occurred before we landed at Detroit and at that city as well, among them being the only passenger who talked English, and who had served as interpreter for the party. He was a strong young man in the prime of life, who had spent some time in America. We were packed into immigrant cars, and a considerable number of deaths occurred in our car before Chicago was reached. While the cholera thus took a heavy toll among the passengers, the Haugen family and a neighbor family from the Old Country, each numbering eight persons, seemed to be immune. Mother was sick, supposedly with the disease, but recovered. It may have been some other ailment not so fatal. The cholera did not originate with the immigrants. The first cases occurring in the country in 1854 seem to have been one at Buffalo and one at St. Louis. There were one or two cases the previous year. Many deaths occurred in Chicago and adjacent country.

While I was serving in the House of Representatives in Washington in 1892 or 1893, cholera raged in Germany, especially in Hamburg; and a matter came to my attention which seemed to solve the mystery of our immunity in 1854. Literature sent to the members of Congress on the subject by medical associations, in connection with proposed quarantine legislation, conveyed the information that any acid is fatal to the cholera germ—the *comma bacillus,* so called. It is, or was, a custom among the country people of our section of Norway, in harvest time or in warm weather generally, to drink whey, or for want of whey, to put vinegar in the water to assuage the thirst. The *comma bacillus* is generally propagated in water. So it was stated in the circulars referred to. Father somehow was on his guard against bad water, and insisted on giving it to us only after mixing it with vinegar. The same was the case with the neighbor family. It also came to us from newspapers, or through circulars, that while thousands of deaths from cholera occurred in Hamburg, no one employed in the breweries in that city died from the disease. Evidently they did not drink the water of the Elbe; and what German working in a brewery would? But, without being conscious of the fact, the two neighbors had evidently hit upon the proper remedy to stand off the fatal disease.

We came on to Beloit. Our final destination was Pierce County, the "Rush River Settlement," so called, where some neighbors had settled a year or two earlier. To get there we were to take steamboat from Galena to Prescott. But there was no railroad to Galena, and people were afraid of the immigrants and cholera. Ole Hei, a farmer living near what is now Orfordville, in Rock County, took us to his place, where we remained only a few days, until we secured lodgment elsewhere. But Ole Hei and two sons died from cholera the same summer. Other deaths occurred in the neighborhood. The Haugen family remained well and healthy, and with the exception of my oldest sister, who died at the age of about forty-five, have all passed the biblical term of three score and ten years. Father died at eighty, and mother had passed ninety-five. She was born January 13, 1809, a month before Lincoln. Speaking of the family health not long ago I said to my sister, older than I, that I thought father had never paid a dollar as doctor's bill for any of the children, and she agreed.

Father soon found employment in the hay and harvest field. Wheat was the prevailing crop in Rock County in those days. A kind neighbor, Ole Gullikson, gave father

permission to build a small log cabin on his farm near his own
double log house. In the small quarters thus prepared the
family of eight were reasonably comfortable and happy during the winter. I visited Rock County in the fall of 1881
during the state campaign, had dinner with Ole Gullikson
and wife, still in their log house, the robust old fellow recit-
ing with much interest and pleasure his own early pioneer
experience and his pleasant recollections of the winter when
he and father often spent the evenings togther. I did not
see the old Viking again, but have a very clear recollection of
his splendid physique and unique Norwegian dialect, which
he had preserved in all its strength and purity. He died
some years ago, a resident of Iowa County, a strong type of
the immigrant of his day, when Norwegian emigration was
almost exclusively from the small landholding class and very
few came from the cities and towns. It is probably safe to
say that among our fellow passengers across the ocean not
half a dozen were from any but rural districts. They were
all from the southern parts of Norway. They came land-
hungry, with a fixed determination to procure independent
homes. Seeking employment was with them a secondary
matter, to secure the maintenance of the family while the
main enterprise was in necessary abeyance. They came to
stay, to become citizens of the country, and with strong
hands and willing hearts to do their share in the "Winning of
the West." The census of 1920, according to press analysis,
shows that the Norwegian immigrant and his immediate descendants hold a larger acreage of agricultural lands according to population than any other class. It is true that in
later years the immigration has shifted, like that from other
European countries, more to the urban population; but the
rural type still prevails throughout the Northwest, where
the bulk of the nationality found its homes.

But we had not reached our destination, which was Pierce County; and in the spring of 1855 the journey was continued. Halvor Hersgard, a neighbor, rigged out a "prairie schooner," into which all our belongings, as well as the members of the family by turns, when not afoot, were taken to Galena. We crossed the Sugar and Pecatonica rivers; one of them was forded, there being no bridge. Shullsburg Prairie was our first view of that kind of wide and level expanse of country, and was the occasion of comment by Mr. Hersgard and father. As we approached Galena we encountered teams hauling lead, or lead ore. Galena on the Fever River was then a Mississippi port, which later had to be abandoned because filled up with the mud of the river. In 1889 the then representative from the district, Mr. Hill, secured a small appropriation to dredge the harbor, but it is not now navigable. Galena was in the fifties quite a distributing center for the Northwest, especially the upper Mississippi and branches, like the St. Croix and the Chippewa. A story well known among the members of the St. Croix County bar ran about as follows: A merchant at Hudson had bought a shipment of groceries from a Galena house, the shipment necessarily including in the interest of his customers a barrel of whiskey. The whiskey did not meet the St. Croix standard, and he refused to pay for it. An action was brought and while the case was on trial in the circuit court the sitting judge ordered a sample of the goods brought into court, so that he and the jury might know whether the defense was justified in refusing payment of a standard article of trade. It is stated that after due examination of the article the judge disposed of the case summarily by saying: "No man can come into my court and collect pay for such damnable stuff as that is." The case was dismissed, no doubt with general approval of jury and bar.

Well, to continue, we took a steamer at Galena and

started up the Mississippi. The boat carried two barges and, although this was as early as May, if not April, the Mississippi was so low that season that the barges were abandoned on some sandbar, probably near the mouth of the Chippewa. It had been an open winter in Rock County, and probably also on the upper streams. We lost much of our household goods. There is no accounting for what an immigrant considered a part of his necessary outfit in going to America in those days, and father had included among his "necessaries" his old and beloved anvil. Being a hard-fisted and reasonably hard-headed man, he did not include the bellows; he preferred the anvil. But, alas, it was lost on the sandbars of the Mississippi. He made a trip later to St. Paul, but not knowing to whom to apply for information and advice the loss remained unsolved and unpaid for.

We landed at Prescott, where we remained three days, waiting for a conveyance to take us to the Rush River settlement some twenty-five miles to the east. Here we saw our first Indians, Sioux camping on the island opposite the village. Prescott was at the time the county seat of Pierce County. It was a rival of Hudson for the trade of the back country, the two being the shipping ports for many years of the principal product of the soil, wheat, which was hauled to the market from twenty-five to thirty miles, generally with oxen. I recollect that in the summer of 1862 I drove a yoke of oxen with a load of wheat to Prescott, and saw five boats following one another land at the wharf to take on wheat. Father was along, but he never took to driving oxen, leaving that to the boys. Oxen were not used as draft animals in our part of Norway.

For the last thirty years, or longer, there has been practically no river traffic on the upper Mississippi. Whether the new government undertaking in that respect will amount to any noticeable competition with railways may be questionable. But railways were not built to St. Paul until about 1866, at any rate not till after the Civil War—or, to use the language adopted by congressional enactment, the War of the Rebellion, which term was severely criticized by southern representatives, aided by some of their Democratic friends from the North. But the term remains as authoritative of the civil conflict.

After waiting three days in Prescott, a Norwegian farmer from Rush River appeared, and we spent a night and a day covering the twenty-five miles—with oxen, of course—to the settlement, where we found temporary lodgment with a former neighbor, Anders A. Bakke. I might as well say that "Bakke" means "hill." "Haugen" also means "The Hill"; it is definite, the suffix "en" being the definite article. The Bakke home was not an elaborate affair. It was a one-room log house, but had a loft, which was turned over to our family and which was reached by outside entrance by means of a ladder. The house had a slab roof, and as rains came on we had the full benefit of the first fresh water before it ran on through to the family below. But we had reached our destination, and the next thing was to look over the adjoining wild territory for desirable land for a permanent home. Nearly all favorable prairie and more or less open land had been taken. The next day after our arrival father took his shotgun and started out on the quest, having received some general information from Mr. Bakke, who was a man of good judgment and had himself secured land well located. But father was interrupted this first day of his land-hunting. He had not gone eighty rods from the house when he encountered an animal he had often heard of, but had never seen before—a deer. He was right in his element and shot the deer in the head and brought it down with his shotgun. The two families had venison for several days. The country in and about the town of Martell consisted largely of spots of prairie, openings, and poplar thickets with plum trees in abundance. The two southern rows of sections were nearly all hardwood of first quality: oak, ash, maple, basswood, and some butternut. There was no walnut and no shell-bark hickory; some smooth-bark hickory of small growth, and ironwood, but mostly poplar on the edges of the heavier timber. After some investigation father selected eighty acres of land of the "opening" class, and a forty of heavy timber, and went to Hudson, where the United States land office was then located, and got his patent from the government, either immediately or soon thereafter, paying the government price of $1.25 per acre. He sold the homestead in the Old Country for six hundred dollars, had paid the passage of eight persons and their maintenance for a year, of course adding some earnings in the meantime; but he paid for the land in cash. How he did it is a mystery, to at least one of his sons. When his estate was administered in 1896, the title to the land was short and simple, only a patent from the government to him. He was a strict observer of Benjamin Franklin's motto: "He who goes a borrowing goes a sorrowing," a motto not so strictly observed by his descendants. We did not get into our own home until the spring of 1857, when a fairly large log house had been constructed with a good "shake" roof, in which the family enjoyed life and a fair amount of prosperity for many years. The farm was gradually enlarged by a few additional acres of clearing each year.

A remarkable change has come over the upper Rush River Valley. A week or so after our landing in the Bakke home (children of that family have all taken the name Anderson) Hans Bakke, a boy of some ten years, was sent on an errand to a sawmill, known as "McCartney's mill," located at the present little burg of New Centerville, on the southern edge of St. Croix County. The river was then a good live stream furnishing sufficient power for the single muley sawmill, which ran for many years, as did other like sawmills and gristmills at the village of Martell and at other places down the stream. Now the river has almost entirely disappeared at New Centerville, except in floods, and the other mills have also been abandoned. Whether the name was given to the stream because of the "rush" growing along it, or because of its rapid current, is a question. About 1850 lumbermen from some point down the Mississippi had done some logging near what became the village of Martell, and had driven their logs down into the Mississippi. They may have found the current strong and have contributed to the naming. Some years ago the village of Ellsworth secured a site and built a generating plant on the river in the town of El Paso, some fifteen miles below New Centerville, and much farther by river, to supply the village with light and power. But it was found that better and more reliable service could be obtained from the Northern States Power Company, and the municipally-owned power has been abandoned.

I have heard much said about the dreariness, poverty, and homesickness of the early immigrants. My recollection does not bear that out. On the contrary, they were as a rule a happy, industrious, and cheerful lot. The hope of seeing their condition improve as time sped, naturally contributed to happiness. There may have been exceptions, of course, but so there no doubt were among the "Yankees" who came West. The community lived largely within itself. They became Americanized in the best sense of self-reliance and self-help. The language was necessarily Norwegian among themselves, and the use of English came about gradually and naturally in the course of time. Many of the men sought employment in the pineries during the winter, and sometimes in the mills and on the river during the summer, but as a rule the summer season was spent in improving and enlarging the farm.   Father took to his former occupation and soon had a blacksmith shop established on the farm.   He loved his anvil.   But being a somewhat devoted sportsman, he did not omit hunting and fishing and the larder was well furnished from both sources.   Deer were quite plentiful and fish abundant in the Rush.   No limit on catch or bag.   Partridges, ducks, and the beautiful wild pigeons came in flocks. A day spent in the woods generally brought at least one deer, and an afternoon on the river in the summer a respectable crate of beautiful speckled trout.   The Kinnickinnick River rising in St. Croix County near Roberts on the Omaha Railroad and running southwesterly through the city of River Falls emptying into Lake St. Croix, has maintained its water flow much better than the Rush.   Both rise in what was originally a fairly open country and were fed from springs, but in the case of the Rush River the springs themselves have gone dry.   Not so with the Kinnickinnick, which is now one of the very best trout streams in the state.   It also furnishes sufficient power for a municipally-owned electric plant successfully operated by the city of River Falls.

While the immediate community of which I write was principally Norwegian, it was not entirely so.   The first settlers in the valley were three Frenchmen: Joe Martell, Roman Kay, and Jacques Dubois.   The last always went by the more familiar name of "Jock," and that name will be found, I believe, on the plat of the village of Martell.   They had been hunters and trappers, and it was commonly reported that Joe Martell had been wounded somewhere "out West" by the Indians, which left him with a stiff elbow. Jock kept up his hunting until the end.   He once wounded a bear a few miles from his home and, pursuing it, came suddenly upon it in the tall grass.   It showed fight.   It was too late to retreat, and old Jock finally ended the struggle with

his bowie-knife. But he was severely injured and was laid
up for some time. I went with father to see him a couple of
days after the occurrence. Jock died in the winter of 1865.
There were few young women of marriageable age in the
community and Jock married a girl of thirteen or fourteen
years, Mary Thompson. The following was told me by one
of her early girl friends, then of River Falls: On calling on
her one day, Mary Thompson surprised her by saying, "Say,
Mary, I got married yesterday." "Married! Whom did
you marry?" "Say, mother, what was his name? Jock Dubois, or Dubois Jock?" William Kay, son of Roman Kay,
still lives on the old homestead on the banks of the river and
has represented the county in the Assembly. Sons or grand-
sons of Joe Martell resided, when I last heard of them, at
Somerset, St. Croix County.

Mr. Thompson had a sawmill on the river and supplied
the neighborhood with the necessary lumber, mostly hardwood. It was said of his one-blade muley saw, that it went
up one week and came down the next. The mill had been in
the ownership or operation of the Pomeroy brothers, and
when the time came to transfer the property a misunderstanding arose as to the ownership of some planks used in
the construction of a bridge, which the Pomeroys proceeded
to take away. Thompson objected, and tried to maintain his
rights by appearing with a gun. But one of the Pomeroys
knocked him down with a scantling and took the gun away.
It was western justice. No harm and no litigation followed.
But I was reminded of the event many years later when I
was called to Mr. Pomeroy's house to draw up some papers,
and Mrs. Pomeroy said to her husband: "You are too easy;
you never stand up for your rights." I chipped in with the
remark: "You are mistaken, Mrs. Pomeroy; I saw Mr.
Pomeroy stand up for his rights once when the other man

came at him with a gun." Mr. Pomeroy looked up surprised, but when I told him that I had as a boy witnessed his
encounter with Thompson he admitted the facts about as
stated. Both parties were respected citizens. On the whole
there was peace and good fellowship in the community.

Language made very naturally a distinction in social in-
tercourse; but neighbors were friendly and helpful to each
other, and a call for a barn-raising or logging bee always
met with hearty response. The threshing became another
social event, with its chicken dinner. The best the housewife
could afford was none too good for these occasions.

Father raised a little wheat the first year of his farming,
but not enough, he thought, to warrant his paying for a "setting," which was a minimum charge for the thresher's outfit.
So he arranged a plank platform and threshed out his few
bushels of wheat with a flail, as he had done in the Old
Country. The winnowing was the same primitive type,
throwing the chaff and wheat across the platform, the chaff
naturally falling by the way, thus separating itself from the
grain. The charge for a "setting" was about five dollars,
and "fives" were not plentiful.

The settlements along the upper Mississippi naturally
began on the land near the river, that being the outlet and
general highway. It also contained more of the prairie and
openings than the back country. But the soil was generally,
if not universally, fertile. The land adjoining the Mississippi is more broken, being cut through by deep valleys of
the little streams in which the country abounds. But there
is little land that can be said to be worthless in the country
between the Chippewa and the St. Croix, except in the northern and more sandy region. The settlements referred to are
prosperous and progressive. Wheat raising practically disappeared as the principal crop about 1878, the chinchbug be-

ing largely the cause. No doubt it was a blessing in disguise, for it turned the farmer's attention to other crops and to dairying, more profitable to himself and to the farm in the end. The immigrant's wife was more than a helpmate; she was as familiar with the hoe and the rake as she was with the towel and the broom.

SCHOOLS

During our first winter in Rock County my sisters had attended school, and I had for a few days, being six years old the following spring. But we had all, including myself, learned to read Norwegian quite readily, and when I went to the English school I had the alphabet by rote and could rattle it off from A to Z. In Martell a primitive schoolhouse had been built. It had a slab roof, some plank seats, no desks, a large box stove with a drum. But no fuel had been provided, and the winter proved to be very cold. The older boys were supposed to cut up slabs and scantlings from the near-by sawmill to keep the teacher and the children from freezing. Our lunches were thawed out in the drum of the stove, and the few children huddled about the red-hot stove in order to be comfortable. This, however, was only for a year or two. A better house was provided, although it, too, during my entire attendance in district school would be condemned by present-day requirements. But we enjoyed things in their simple state. Only one desk was provided, and those who practiced penmanship had to change about. The teacher furnished her own schedule. While this naturally took some time for a new teacher, it necessarily made her study the children as to progress and general capacity and helped to develop her own ability as a governing force. The teachers were young and inexperienced, but the scholars were in the primary classes, and on the whole the situation was fairly well met. Reading and spelling were the main studies, and some of us at least became very good spellers. Spelling schools, where children and grown-ups from several districts met, spurred on to rivalry, until Sanders' *Spelling Book* was perfectly familiar. Arithmetic and geography were studied to some extent, but grammar was a hidden science to teacher as well as pupil.

Parochial schools in the Norwegian Lutheran settlements were taught in the homes of the settlers before public schoolhouses were erected, the school moving from one home to another as was convenient; the teacher as a rule lived for the time being with the family entertaining the school. Men taught these schools, as had been the custom in the Old Country. The catechism and church history were the principal subjects. No doubt the children of these immigrants were far better versed in biblical history than were the children of the "native Americans." I remember a little personal incident. An old lady (native) fell in company with my sisters and myself on our way to school one morning, and asked me who was the oldest man that ever lived. I answered readily, "Methuselah." "How old was he?" "Nine hundred and sixty-nine years." "No," said the lady, "he was 999 years, lacking only one year of a thousand." I insisted on 969, but was emphatically overruled.

We had in our district school a good mixture of nationalities: mostly Norwegians, but some Americans, Irish, French, and at least one German family. The melting pot was doing its work, and all the pupils lived together in the best of harmony and good will, which continued throughout their mature years. In an adjoining district every family was Norwegian, and English was not acquired so easily. I had occasion to observe this when I taught in that district.

The children all persisted in using Norwegian on the playground. I tried to make them use English. I had taught Norwegian parochial school in the district for a couple of months before teaching the district school proper. At the time (this was in 1871), the law permitted the teaching of one hour in some other language than English. The school board asked me to do this; but I told them that what their children needed was English, and that five months' school, which was all they had provided for, ought to be devoted entirely to the use of English. They yielded to my argument. Time takes care of the question of language; and I find now in visiting that very community that English is used commonly, if not universally, by those very children and their descendants. The services in the Norwegian churches were then exclusively in the mother tongue. Now both languages are used, at least half of the services being conducted in English. While there is some effort, especially among the foreign press, to preserve the old language, it is easy to see that it is only a matter of time when it will be forgotten. The recent immigration law will hasten it. Talking to a largely Norwegian audience in Chicago on the seventeenth of May, 1893, I called attention to the fact that the change was then taking place. In one Norwegian church in that city English had then been introduced, and in only one. Today all the so-called Norwegian churches in Madison use both languages, and it is the same throughout the country. It is a matter that takes care of itself in the natural course of events, if let alone. My experience has been that the foreign-language press is as well informed, and in its editorials frequently better informed, than the purely English of comparatively the same standard of circulation. Editors of the foreign-language papers were and are, as a rule, men of a more liberal education than the majority of the English press.

INDIANS

Until the Indian outbreak in Minnesota in 1862, Sioux Indians used to cross the Mississippi and spend the winters hunting in the "big woods" of Pierce and St. Croix counties. They came to father's shop and generally came to the house to get something to eat; and they never went away hungry. They always seemed to be hungry when they arrived. They were a peaceable lot, and there was no charge or rumor against any of them, of any theft or other offense. They would not talk English if it could be avoided. I recollect falling in with a half a dozen of them on the way to school, when one of the younger members of the gang edged up to us children, evidently fearing that we might be afraid of them and talked English with us quite readily. The country west of the Chippewa seems to have been in a sense neutral territory between the Sioux and Chippewa. We never saw any of the Chippewa in our neighborhood. They were numerous in and about Menomonie and Eau Claire, and to the north. We were on "Carver's Grant," which had been given by the Sioux to Jonathan Carver. The Sioux were evidently liberal when it came to the lands of the Chippewa.

There was an old rumor that there had been somewhat of a battle between the two tribes at some point on Rush River a dozen miles or so below our settlement, but, if true, I have never seen anything to substantiate it. The Sioux never appeared on the east side of the Mississippi after the Minnesota outbreak. The winter previous to it they were with us, and father changed some of their flintlocks to the percussion-cap lock. I have one of the old flints still in my possession, as a relic of their last visit. The cone-shaped bare ironwood poles forming the framework of their tents remained for some time on their camping ground in what was known as the Big Cooley.

EARLY OCCUPATIONS

One of the occupations of the boys, and men too, about 1860 in the summer time was to dig ginseng, which was quite plentiful in the hardwood belt. Men dug as much as thirty pounds in a day, and sold it at six cents a pound. In the summer of 1861 I went with three men and two other boys to Maple Springs in the present town of Eau Galle, Dunn County, and dug ginseng for a month. The men—an Irishman, a German, and a Yankee—dug by the pound. The boys received six dollars and board for the month, the first money I earned. The man financing the ginseng enterprise no doubt made a good profit.

The boys raised in the timber settlements were all accustomed to finding their way home somewhat instinctively. When eight years old I lived with a settler beyond whose house there was not another for miles to the south and southwest. It was part of my duty to go after the cattle, and they sometimes strayed away for miles. In order that I might not get lost Mr. Heyerdahl gave me his compass for a guide, and I never felt any alarm. I knew that by going north or east I should reach settlers. But we were also taught to use the primitive guide of the moss on the north side of the trees in lieu of compass. We were all taught to work, and what was true of our settlement was true of like situations elsewhere.

As a farmer boy I necessarily took part in such work as my age warranted, and left home early. When eight years old I spent most of a year with Mr. Heyerdahl, referred to above. Mr. Heyerdahl was a man of more than usual education from the Old Country; had studied English, German, and other languages. While this kept me out of school practically for the year, I had the advantage of additional books in his home—Norwegian books, of course, which satisfied to some extent my reading hunger. There were no circulating libraries in those days, and the settlers did not, as a rule, bring with them many books. While at this home I was often left with Mrs. Heyerdahl, a most excellent and kind woman, as Mr. Heyerdahl was the assessor of the town and away on his duties for days, the town then consisting of three townships. Much of it, however, was entirely vacant and unoccupied. An incident occurred in the early summer. Hogs, like cattle, strayed into the woods. One day we heard the squeal of a hog, which alarmed Mrs. Heyerdahl. I think I made the remark that it must be a bear. But without hesitating I immediately went to the aid of the hog. True enough, it was a bear, and I ran up close to it in the high grass where it was regaling itself on very fresh pork. It might have had boy for desert, but was evidently as much surprised as the boy. Or it may have had a full meal. It slunk away, which reassured me; but do not think for a moment that I pursued it. I felt no fear at the time, but really feared to pass that place later. I reported to Mrs. Heyerdahl, and was sent to the neighbors to give the alarm. The bear was shot a day or two later when it came back to finish its repast; it was a mother bear with cubs, but the latter were not captured. Bears were not uncommon. They were not, as a rule, dangerous unless wounded. I never heard of one attacking a person. There were wolves and a very few foxes along the Mississippi, but we were never molested by them; I never saw a wolf or a fox in the wild state.

THE CIVIL WAR

The Scandinavians were strongly opposed to slavery, and quite naturally intensely loyal when the news reached the North of the firing on Fort Sumter. I recollect that we were dragging a new breaking when a neighbor—Mr. Lawrence, I think— came cross-lots to tell father that war had broken out. We soon had the news confirmed in the Norwegian papers, which father always kept and assiduously read. A few days later, however, we were assured that the war would soon be settled. A Norwegian neighbor came to tell us that he had seen at Prescott three hundred soldiers from Fort Snelling going down the river on a boat; and he added assuringly, "There was one Norwegian among them, too." If the two hundred and ninety-nine could not manage the rebels, that Norwegian would. A sentiment not to be deprecated; a kind of family pride. More Norwegians went South later, and many of those from our immediate neighborhood still rest in southern soil, among them my boyhood friend Hans Bakke and brother Christopher. They died with many others on Island No. 10 in the Mississippi, from malarial or typhoid fever, and as that island has been washed away their graves have gone with it. Quite a number of those enlisting were fresh from the Old Country, and perhaps for that reason less immune to the southern climate than the native Americans. Some brought with them military experience. My first public service was acting as interpreter for an agent of the government taking a census of those in our town subject to the impending draft, for which service I received twenty-five cents and got scolded by a neighbor woman for handing in the name of a man who lived at her house. This man was drafted, and perhaps killed in battle, as he was among those "unaccounted for." Father had passed the military age, and his boys had not reached it.

When the election of 1864 came on, there was much politics in the air. Lincoln was strong among the foreign element in our section. There were, of course, exceptions. The Norwegian Lutheran Church had before the war become affiliated with the German Lutherans, and the young students of divinity among them had been going to the German Lu-

theran Seminary at St. Louis to complete their theological
studies. Missouri was a slave state, and some of the leaders
in the church took the position that slavery was sanctioned
by the Bible and that it was not a sin *per se* to own slaves.
A bitter controversy on the subject followed in the press,
generally with the laymen on one side against slavery, and
some of the clergy defending it. The *per se* argument did
not appeal to the laity. It was too subtle.

Time passed on and with it the war. Soldiers came home
on furlough, or because of sickness. In the winter of 1863-
1864 a couple of soldiers of the Second Minnesota, after
taking part in several battles, had reënlisted and been
granted a short furlough. They came to our neighborhood
to visit relatives, and when they were going back to their
regiment I took them to Red Wing, from which point they
went by stage on the ice down the Mississippi to La Crosse,
to which place the railroad had then been extended. Such
were the means of travel. The stage line in Wisconsin was
running from Sparta through Eau Claire, Menomonie, and
Hudson to St. Paul; but Red Wing was as near to us as
Hudson, and in the winter time the road was preferred, although for much of the way it was a mere trail leading
through the heavy forest.

At the age of fourteen I was confirmed in the Lutheran
Church. This ceremony was often considered a kind of
manumission among the Lutherans, the boys being then permitted to leave home and seek employment. While I had
some ambition to continue my school studies, such as they
were, the family was large and the income scant. I did the
usual farm work in the spring, harvest, and other times. In
the threshing season I worked with the machine and was entrusted to measure the grain as it came from the spout, which
was done by using two half-bushel measures, and by moving

a peg on a board fastened to the side of the separator for every bushel. This was generally a man's job.

There was at the time a stave factory located about two miles south of the village of Ellsworth, and in the spring of 1864 I went there to work, "butting" staves until harvest time, when the factory shut down, the men seeking better pay in the harvest fields. I worked there again two years later, first "edging" and later driving a span of mules hauling staves to Diamond Bluff and Prescott to be shipped to the flouring mills at Minneapolis and elsewhere. Two teams made the round trip each day to Diamond Bluff, where we fed teams and drivers, took a swim in the Mississippi, and returned. We were tempted to a foolhardy undertaking one day by challenging each other to swim across the river. The challenge was unhesitatingly accepted and the trip safely made, but the stream at that place has considerable current and carried us down at least half a mile. We made our return along the bank in that original costume that Adam was ashamed of. But there was no angel at the gate to censure us, and no criticism.

I was an interested spectator at the polls in the fall of 1864. Some soldiers were home on furlough and voted, as that was permitted at the time, regardless of their legal residence—a privilege accorded the soldiers only. I have the date clearly in mind, for the next day I walked to Menomonie a distance of fully forty miles, in company with a man about twenty-six years old. It snowed all day and I was probably the most tired boy in Wisconsin that evening when we reached our destination. I fell in behind my companion, so as to have the advantage of stepping in his tracks. We landed about nine o'clock in the "shanty," which was the living quarters of the employees of Knapp, Stout, and Company for their mill hands. But when my companion suggested that we go over to the "kitchen" to get something to eat, I followed, although to remain seated where I was or to go to bed would have been preferred. I hired for the winter at sixteen dollars a month, which was generally a boy's wages at the time. Of course it included board and lodging, with a plentiful supply of "cooties" thrown in. That classical term had not been invented for the nuisance at that time. In Knapp, Stout, and Company's supplies they passed under the vulgar name of "graybacks."

The wage of the common laborer at the time was twenty-six dollars per month, teamsters and choppers about thirty dollars. And that remained as a rule the wage for several years, although the paper money after the war was very much depreciated. Along about 1866 we hauled wheat some twenty-five miles to Hudson and sold it for sixty-five to seventy cents a bushel; but merchandise was by no means correspondingly cheap. The paper money fell to less than fifty cents in gold at one time, and caused an inflation of prices—something the Greenbackers advocated at a later period. Still there was less complaint of hard times than at present. On the "drive" in the spring and in the harvest field the wage ran about three dollars per day. But it meant a long day—as early as the dew would allow until dark in harvest, and on the river from daylight to dark.

The Menomonie sawmills were well patronized by Scandinavians and other newcomers; had been and continued to be as long as the pine held out and kept the mills occupied. Knapp, Stout, and Company were at the time I went there one of the largest lumber concerns in the country. They denuded the northern part of Dunn County and most of Barron County of its rich white pine forests. No regard was paid to the enormous waste. The gangsaw with its heavy blades made sawdust of a great part of the log. This was to some extent remedied later when the thinner band-saw was introduced. The slabs and scantlings were burned as waste, except for a small portion used by residents as fuel.

For some time I was put to burning up this waste, and, as it was getting cold, had the luxury of a good fire at my command. After the Holidays I worked with other boys and young men packing and edging shingles. I believe our day was eleven hours—at least ten and a half. There were no Saturday afternoons off in those days, nor at any time while I was engaged in manual labor. A holiday off was entirely unheard of. Knapp, Stout, and Company had written contracts with their men. They were hired for a certain number of months, and the terms were that if a man did not serve his full time he was "docked" four dollars a month. No payment was made until the term expired. So that meant a reduction of four dollars a month for the life of the contract if a man quit. It was said that Knapp, Stout, and Company docked a man if he died before the term of his service expired. The company itself adhered strictly to its obligations, and there was no disappointment when the service had been fully performed; its credit was always good and the cash was ready. Along in the spring I was "promoted" from the shingle mill to drive a yoke of oxen and deliver fuel from the refuse of the mill around town. Menomonie was not a large village at the time, and a great part of the population lived on the west side of the river, mainly in houses belonging to the company. The food was good and there was plenty of it. Strangers looking for employment were never refused a seat at the "kitchen" table, whether engaged or not. I remember soldiers on furlough, or for some reason excused from service for a time, being at the table for dinner; and some Indians also were free guests. The latter were quite numerous at Menomonie at the time, but I do not recollect ever seeing any of them at work about the mills.

In the "shanty" there was a large room where the men spent their evenings. There was no brawling, and on the whole the company was quite congenial. I often spent the evening playing checkers with one of the bosses, when he learned that I could play the game. There was no gambling, and no saloons near the mill. There were plenty of them over where the present city is located. I never entered one the entire time of my service, nor was I ever invited to enter one; and I believe that was true of other boys of my age. The men seemed to have the protection of the boys in mind in that respect. The hours of labor were strictly enforced, and any absence meant loss of pay. Old "Cap." Wilson was the general boss at the mill, and although he had recently been converted and baptized I have distinctly in mind a good scolding with considerable choice profanity intermixed because the boys in the shingle mill had placed knotty shingles on the outside of the bunch. There was no objection to the knots if they were not in sight.

The only request mother made when I left for Menomonie was that I should not enlist until I returned home. But in the meantime the war ended in April, and her mind was no doubt very much relieved. I came home in May with over ninety dollars saved out of the ninety-six dollars received for my winter's work. The only luxury I had indulged in was a ticket to Robinson's circus, the first circus I ever saw.

In 1866 at the end of the season at the stave factory, harvesting came on. After that and threshing I went to Stillwater and engaged to pull an oar on a lumber raft down the St. Croix and Mississippi, taking about a month to reach its destination, Albany, Illinois. Handling an oar on a raft was no boy's work. The blade of the oar was a plank about six feet in length, two inches thick at the butt and thinning to half an inch at the end. The stem or handle was a sapling some six inches where it was attached to the blade, and tapering to the handle end. The raft was not propelled, but just drifted with the stream, the oars being used only to keep it in the current. The oar was dipped into the water with a swing so that the rower held it at arm's length above his head and walked across the space of some fifteen feet with each "stroke" of the oar. Sinking the six-foot oar was a trick, extremely difficult at first, but when acquired was performed quite easily. By the time we had passed the mouth of the St. Croix at Prescott I had learned the trick, and enjoyed the trip down the river. The raft just drifting with the current gave considerable leisure. The day lasted from daybreak to dark. A Mississippi raft was composed of cribs usually sixteen by thirty-two feet, and ten cribs in length by ten wide, or one hundred cribs, making the length three hundred and twenty feet and the width one hundred and sixty. In later years the rafts were propelled by a steamboat, but at the time referred to, that aid to their navigation was resorted to only through Lakes St. Croix and Pepin. These lakes are as beautiful inland waters as any in the Northwest. Their shores rise in places some four hundred or five hundred feet above the water. I think it was about this time that Horace Greeley, a passenger on a steamer on the river, remarked prophetically that it would not be many years before there would be railroads on both banks of the Mississippi; this we have seen realized for more than forty years. River traffic was too slow. On returning I came back up the river to Reads Landing at the mouth of the Chippewa, and took a small steamer—I think the *Billy Wilson*—for Dunnville, a little village about a mile above the mouth of the Red Cedar where it empties into the Chippewa. Dunnville was the port where Knapp, Stout, and Company received their provisions and goods for Menomonie. From there the carrying was done by means of several yoke of

oxen before a large wagon with tires six inches wide, to float
it over the sandy road between Dunnville and Menomonie,
the trip taking two days. The accommodations for raftsmen
on the boats were letting them take care of themselves on the
lower deck, and as my trip was in November, the nights were
generally passed as near to the boiler and engine as the fire-
man and engineer would permit.

During the month of November of that year, 1866, I
went into the pinery on the upper Willow River to work
for Silas Staples, of Hudson. This Staples was a brother of
the lumber king of the day, of Stillwater, Minnesota. The
crew engaged at Hudson walked up through New Richmond to a point some eighteen miles farther on, where we
established ourselves for the winter by building a camp with
necessary accommodations for the oxen; no horses were used.
The camp for the men, a crew of sixteen, was a log house
with a fireplace in the center used for cooking as well as
heating—a large opening left in the center of the roof, with
a short elevation of slats and clay, serving as chimney. The
fireplace in the center was always open and there the cooking was done. It was living-room, kitchen, and bedroom,
all in one. There were bunks along both the long sides, and
a long table across the end. Pots and kettles were piled
away in one of the corners. We were quite comfortable. Before retiring for the night several logs were put on the fireplace to keep the fire going all night. Sometimes it took two
or even three men to carry in one of these sticks of wood.
Occasionally one would roll off during the night, and hustle
us out of the bunk to keep it from setting the bunk on fire.
The food was simple but good—no coffee, no sugar, no milk,
and no fresh meats with the exception of a deer brought
down by one of the men. But we had beans and pork
a-plenty; salt meats, beans every meal, tea, and blackstrap—
the last used instead of sugar. One thing not to be forgotten

was hot biscuits every meal, baked before the open fire in a tin baker. Far different from the lumber camp of today, primitive in its arrangement but evoking no complaining or criticism. The boss, son of the proprietor, lived with the men. The crew were clean, and not a cootie or other bug was discovered all winter or on the drive in the spring— something unusual for a lumber camp. The camp must have been a short distance above the St. Croix County line in Polk County. It was some eight or ten miles to the northeast of the present village of Deer Park, which was a deer park in fact in those days, an old German of some means indulging his fancy by keeping a number of live deer in a very high enclosure of several acres.

The pay was twenty-six dollars a month for general labor; thirty dollars for teamsters and choppers, the latter felling the trees only. The teamster for our camp—or more properly the ox driver—was an old Maineite, Charles Weston, a highly respectable citizen of St. Croix County for many years. The tree was cut and marked for the proper number of logs and their length. No logs were cut less than eleven inches at the top; all white pine. The swamper cleared the way for the teams. The barker pealed the bark off the part of the tree that would drag on the ground, as the whole tree after clearing it of branches and the top was hauled to the landing, one end on a pair of bobs and the other, irrespective of whether it was butt or top, dragging. The sawing was done on the landing—"sawing on the landing," this operation was called. I sawed on the landing all winter, handling my end of a cross-cut saw and filing and setting the saw in the evening, my companion having no knack in that respect. Mr. Weston had brought with him into camp some of Scott's novels, which I read with much interest. It was the only reading at hand, and my first ac-

quaintance with Scott and that class of literature. I had
read previously the poem *The Lady of the Lake.*

THE DRIVE

As spring approached, preparations were made for the
drive, always an interesting part of a lumberman's life.
Nearly all of the crew engaged for it. Additional recruits
were added, and the drive began early in April. The pay
was three dollars a day. To be properly prepared it was
necessary to have a good pair of driving boots, well caulked,
in order to be able to keep on top of logs made slippery by
removal of the bark. I had had some experience on logs
during my early days in the Martell school, which was located so near the millpond that all the boys became adepts
in riding even small logs—any log that would carry a boy.
For that reason I was placed at the front to keep the logs
moving, and never did any "sacking," which meant wading
in the water and clearing up the rear of the drive by getting
the stranded logs back into the stream. I had one good
wetting the second day of the drive, when the water was icy
cold. But fortunately no one saw it, so I was saved from being guyed. It was always a matter of merriment to see one
fall in. I had on three woolen shirts at the time; I took them
off and wrung them out, put them on again, and wore them
for three weeks, and never suffered a cold or other inconvenience from the mishap. We slept in tents. The blankets
were sewed together so that we were practically under one
blanket, the entire crew, the wet and the dry. Steam would
rise when the blanket was thrown off. The working day was
from daylight to dark in order to take advantage of the high
water while it lasted. Hot pork and beans and biscuit were
carried to us on the river for two meals of the four each day.
Falling in was always considered a joke on the victim. We

had with us a young man from Rock County, Sam White-head, who had his first experience on the river; an active, alert young fellow. Early in the drive Sam and I were riding down the stream, each on a log, I being a little in advance. We reached a swift current or rapid, when Sam called out: "Look out, Nils, that's where Hank went in yesterday." I looked out and passed in safety into calmer water. Not hearing further from Sam, I turned and saw him struggling to get back onto his log, which was no easy task. But it was all in a day's work. I never saw Sam after that spring; he was a good fellow and companion.

A rule of the river was that when logs of several owners became mixed the drive was conducted jointly, the expense being divided in accordance with the ratio of ownership. There was a struggle on the part of those farthest up the river to get into the drive ahead. There was one camp above those of Staples. But our drive escaped ahead. We came on down through New Richmond and Burkhardt and into the backwaters of the Willow at Hudson.

I have given a brief account of some of my various experiences as a manual laborer, undoubtedly the experience in the main of hundreds of other boys of the times. There was no age limit on the employment of boys at the time. Under present laws I would have been prevented from working in the mills and factories because of my age. But it was not a loss in my case. I saved a large part of my earnings, and had an experience not without its value. It is a question whether boys are benefited by being prevented from engaging in work not injurious to health! Education is of course to be encouraged. But many boys must of necessity at some time or other do manual labor, and if their hands are not trained to some extent in early boyhood, it is a serious loss to them in more mature years. It is no doubt due to that fact that country boys are often given preference over city boys.

I had not lost sight of the fact that I desired to pursue further my own schooling. I loved to read, and had some desire for mathematics, but nothing definite in view.

CHAPTER II

I had not during all these years abandoned a desire to acquire some further education. I loved to read and had read all the books of our family's limited library—not many, but more than those of any neighbor. I had as a boy read the Bible aloud of evenings from Genesis to Revelations, including the Apocrypha, and most of it more than once. I had saved a little money and had invested it in a quarter-section of land.

A young man recently graduated from the theological department of the University of Christiania came to America in 1856 and was called to the pastorate of the Lutheran Church of our settlement. This was the Reverend Lauritz Larsen. He adapted himself without hesitation to his unfamiliar surroundings, something an educated European frequently if not generally failed to do. Mr. Larsen became popular in the settlement. But he remained there only a couple of years, being called as an associate professor to Concordia College, the German theological seminary at St. Louis. Later he became the head of Luther College, Decorah, Iowa. He was enterprising and active, and had much to do with the creation of that school. There was probably not another person in the country at the time who possessed his peculiar fitness for that position, which he filled so admirably to the end of his active life.

In the summer of 1868 Professor Larsen visited his old parishioners and called on my parents. Addressing himself

to me he inquired why I could not come to Decorah. While
that matter may have suggested itself, it had never before
been put to me so squarely. I apologized for my unpre-
paredness, which he brushed aside with the assurance that I
would average with the majority of the new students of the
institution. I was then nineteen and had not finished what
is now known as the grades. We knew nothing of "grades"
in our district school. The result, however, was that I entered Luther College the following September. The full
course was six years, the first two years being in fact pre-
paratory to the college course proper. The classes bore the
Latin numbers *Sexta* to *Prima;* the *Sextas* were the begin-
ners. I took the general course, not having any definite profession in view. I was not then or at any time urged to prepare for the ministry. The course of studies was largely lin-
guistic, and much attention was paid to the classics. It was
the continental European method. Norwegian and English
naturally predominated, but German and Latin were also
pursued the first year; and students were required to translate into Norwegian or English, generally the former, Norwegian being used exclusively in the churches of the Norwegian settlements at the time and it seemed to be taken
for granted that it always would be. Mathematics, history,
and other college studies had a share in the program, but
most attention was devoted to the languages. It was an excellent training in grammar. I must have more than held
my own, for at the end of the year I was the only one of a
class of forty-five who was advanced over the succeeding
class year; so that at the beginning of the college year in
1869 I entered *Quarta,* which may be considered the first
college year proper. Greek and algebra were then added to
the studies. With two exceptions the faculty were men edu-

cated at and graduates of the university of Norway. The
exceptions were Professor Schmidt, a German divine; and
an attorney of Decorah, Mr. Bergh, who specialized in English and mathematics. They were all capable men and devoted to the duties assigned to them. Professor Larsen had
a remarkable faculty for teaching ancient and European history generally. His memory of events and the relations of
the different dynastic families was exceptional. He did not
lack in the heroic, and was a great admirer of Alexander
the Great, Julius Caesar, Gustavus Adolphus, Charles the
Twelfth, and other hero warriors. I think he did not have
any admiration for Napoleon; considered him "the scourge
of Europe." Perhaps Ludwig's *Napoleon* is more impartial
and just. I acknowledge with respect and gratitude my indebtedness to Luther College for whatever education I may
afterwards have achieved. It laid the foundation. The
study of languages was to me very interesting. I believe to
some extent with Goethe: "Er kennt keine Sprache, der
nur seine eigne kennt" ("He knows no language, who knows
only his own").

The purpose of Luther College was to give primary education to young men who might later study for the Lutheran
ministry. As I did not intend to enter the ministry I did
not return to Decorah in the fall of 1870, but entered what
was called Hinckley's Military Academy at River Falls,
largely because I wanted to get more closely in touch with
English educational methods, as I had teaching in mind,
temporarily at least, and did not know whether my acquire-
ments would secure me the necessary certificate. I think
"Military" was in the title of the school, but cannot account
for the word except that at one time Mr. Hinckley had for
a short period been a cadet at West Point. It was a board-

ing school for young men; coeducational, however, the young
ladies living in private homes. Most of the students were
aspiring to sufficient education to teach in the common
schools. Among them were a few who afterwards acquired
some prominence. William Lauder was for many years
judge of one of the district courts in North Dakota and now
lives at Wahpeton in that state. Edgar Willard Nye—later
known all over the country as "Bill Nye"—and his brother
Frank were among the students. Frank is now judge of the
district court of Minneapolis. He has served as prosecuting
attorney, and also as member of Congress from the Minneapolis district, an able lawyer, level-headed and popular.
He was also for one year a member of the Wisconsin legislature as assemblyman from Polk County. He is a better
public speaker in the general acceptance of the term than
was his brother Ed. Ed, as we knew him, was always quaint
and humorous. The Nye boys were raised on a farm about
five miles northeast of the city of River Falls, in the town
of Kinnickinnick, St. Croix County, both splendid fellows
and good comrades.

BILL NYE

It was some years later, after settling in Wyoming, that
Ed took the pen name of "Bill Nye." While I was stenographer in the circuit court Edgar served as a juror one term
in St. Croix County and we roomed together, thus renewing
our former intimate relations. Both the brothers studied
law in the offices of attorneys at Hudson. While Frank
became a good lawyer, Ed did not seem to take to legal
studies. After reading law a year with Baker and Spooner
in Hudson he spent some time in the office of Bingham and
Jenkins, leading attorneys at Chippewa Falls. The humorous side of his character was developing, if not the legal.

His jokes were frequently at his own expense. It was humor rather than wit, for the latter sometimes stings. Along that line the following may be related: Court was in session at Durand. Ed appeared on the scene and requested me to ask the judge to appoint a committee of members of the bar to examine him, as he wanted to be admitted to practice. The committee was appointed and Ed examined in the usual manner of the times; but he failed. He continued his studies. One day in July a year or so later as I was driving out of the livery stable at River Falls to attend court, then about to meet in special session at Prescott, Ed hailed me and rode with me to Prescott. He was examined again but with the same result. He made the remark, "I am going to be examined in every county in the circuit." He did not, however, follow out that threat, but shortly thereafter moved to Laramie, Wyoming. There he developed his unusual aptitude as a humorist. It seems he also practiced law there. He must have sent me the local paper, the *Boomerang,* in which he gave an account of his experience as an attorney. After stating that he hired an office over the livery stable, he went on to say that he hung out his shingle and began to practice law, "although I had been warned by the authorities in Wisconsin not to undertake such a thing."

River Falls had before the Hinckley Academy a high school now known as the "Old Seminary," which to some extent furnished teachers to the neighboring common schools. It was thus at an early date a little educational center. Hinckley himself had only a mediocre education, but he had two excellent assistants, Mr. Cady and Mr. Baker, both graduates of eastern institutions. Mr. Baker was until recently, and may be yet, principal of one of the high schools in St. Paul. Mr. Cady served as county superintendent in Pierce County; afterwards entered the ministry in the

Methodist Church; moved to Illinois; and died some years
ago, being at the time presiding elder of his district. I read
Sallust's "Conspiracy of Cataline" in Latin with Mr. Cady
and also some Latin poetry, and found him a proficient and
interesting teacher. These early educational institutions at
River Falls no doubt had their influence in securing for it
the location of the state normal school.

After a few months at the Academy I hesitatingly met
with the superintendent of the county, Charles Smith, to secure the necessary credentials to teach. I did not feel too
confident, and by the looks on his face I was not reassured.
He may have been disappointed in finding only one appli-
cant, or in finding that one, for he remarked that there were
more teachers than schools in the county already. I came
back with the remark that I had the school and all I asked
of him was an examination. We went together to the schoolhouse of the place, but having failed to get the key made our
entry through a window, dragging our long bodies into the
room. He was six feet four, beating me by three inches.
He was my senior by ten years. My examination proving
entirely satisfactory, we formed a friendship that continued
until his death about ten years ago. He was judge of the
superior court of Douglas County at the time of his death.

After a year spent partly in teaching, I returned to
Luther College in the autumn of 1871. A few months
after the opening of that school year I received a letter from
Mr. Smith saying that he had recommended me as teacher
to the officers of one of the best country schools in the county,
a purely American district near the city of Prescott, and asking me to consider it seriously; compensation forty-five dollars a month, which was about the peak of compensation for
country teachers at the time. I submitted the matter to the
president, Professor Larsen, who urged me to continue my

studies and complimented me on my progress. But the lure of the forty-five dollars per month and the attractiveness of the district, with which I was quite familiar, were too great and I said that I did not think of entering the ministry in any event. Professor Larsen said that the Lutheran Church would in a few years have several educational institutions, and he considered me, in view of my progress, as well fitted to head one of them. That was complimentary, but the prospect remote. I had not forgotten Mr. Smith's suggestion that I study law. So I severed my connection with "Luther" and did not see the old college again until 1903. It has been an excellent institution for its purpose; its system of education thorough and discipline kindly but efficient for the students' best welfare. I want to add that they STUDIED. They also had sufficient time for healthy recreation and sports, and have furnished very successful baseball teams. I taught four months in the school secured through Mr. Smith, and the district in which I had formerly taught was kind enough to put off its term until the end of that time, when I went without interruption into that, thus teaching continuously for seven months. Mr. Smith taught in Clifton Hollow, an adjoining district, and we frequently met and discussed plans for the future.

Having determined to take up law, I consulted Baker and Spooner, leading attorneys at Hudson, as to the best school to attend. They recommended the University of Michigan at Ann Arbor. The Wisconsin University law department was then in its infancy, while Michigan, with Thomas M. Cooley, then chief justice of the state supreme court, at the head, had a high standing throughout the country. So in the fall of 1872 I went there together with two companions, also teachers from Pierce County, and took up the study of law, beginning naturally with Cooley's

Blackstone and Kent's *Commentaries.* The law faculty
consisted of Judge Cooley as head, Judge Campbell, also of
the supreme court, and two practicing attorneys from Detroit—Kent and Walker—as assistants.   The instruction
during the first year was in the form of lectures, the quiz-
zing being reserved for the second or senior year.   When
Chief Justice Winslow of our supreme court published *The
Story of a Great Court,* in which he spoke in highest terms
of his predecessor, Chief Justice Dixon, I took occasion to
say to him that in his lectures to the class Judge Cooley in
quoting one of Dixon's decisions referred to him as one of
the greatest jurists of the United States; at this Judge
Winslow seemed very much pleased. Judge Cooley had a
wonderful memory and as a rule lectured without referring
to notes, frequently citing volume and page of decisions, not
only of the court of which he was a member, but of the federal courts and those of other states. We did not take much
part in the social life of the University, but devoted ourselves
to study. By way of diversion some of us took up shorthand,
and by practice in taking notes from the lectures became
reasonably proficient. The class of which I was a member—
one hundred and twenty-six in number—graduated in the
spring of 1874; many of us went to Detroit and were admitted to practice in the courts of Michigan, and then separated to all parts of the Union.   Students come to Michigan from all sections, and veterans on both sides of the conflict of ten years before met and in friendly converse spoke
of taking part on opposite sides in the same battles. This
I witnessed personally.

During the winter preceding graduation I had frequent
correspondence with Mr. Smith, then practicing law at Prescott. He had a better opinion of River Falls as a growing
town and had been in conference with Mr. Morse—who was

the editor of the River Falls *Journal* and practiced law on the side, principally in justice court—with reference to forming a partnership and taking me into the firm. I had no definite plans, except possibly teaching in case of necessity, and fell in with the suggestion. We thus became residents of the prosperous little city and hung out our "shingle." Mr. Smith and I lived at the Commercial Hotel, where we ate at the same table, slept in the same bed, and played croquet in the back yard on summer evenings.

I had no intention other than to pursue the study and practice of law. But the legislature had during its recent session enacted a law authorizing the appointment of a shorthand reporter in the Eighth Circuit, then presided over by Judge H. L. Humphrey of Hudson. It was a new departure in that part of the state. Previously the judge had taken copious notes of testimony during trials, with frequent interruptions which delayed the proceedings. The firm of Morse, Smith, and Haugen was not crowded with a "cloud of clients," as Mr. Hayden of Eau Claire said about his office. My funds were running low. Judge Humphrey was approached by Mr. Smith and I was appointed to the newly created position, in which I continued for seven years, principally in the Eighth Circuit, but in addition for a part of the time also in the Eleventh, which embraced the northern part of the state bordering on Lake Superior, and on the south taking in Polk and Barron counties. The pay was seven dollars a day for actual attendance, leaving less than five dollars after paying hotel and traveling expenses. After a few years it was raised to ten dollars. Attorneys and court had to adjust themselves to the new method. A murder case, the State *vs.* Long, was one of the first cases I reported. It was tried in Chippewa County, Wheeler and Marshall defending. After an all-day trial and examination of witnesses, Mr. Wheeler asked me if I could let him have a transcript of the evidence in the morning. I had to tell him that it would take several days to make the transcript. Mr. Wheeler was a very adroit and clever attorney in jury trials, far more so than his partner, who served with distinction for many years as judge of the state supreme court. It was no doubt a happy combination, Wheeler for the facts, Marshall for the law.

I naturally became well acquainted with the members of the bar. Besides the firm mentioned, there was Bingham and Jenkins, also of Chippewa Falls. Bartlett and Hayden, and Meggett and Teall were the two leading law firms of Eau Claire; E. B. Bundy, and the firm of Hunt and Freeman, at Menomonie; Hudson had Baker and Spooner, and Wilson and Glover. Wilson later practiced in St. Paul, I think as a partner of Cushman K. Davis, governor of Minnesota and later United States Senator. There were of course other good attorneys in the circuit, but the firms mentioned were somewhat outstanding in their practice.

Judge Humphrey had been on the bench for a number of years, and had the confidence of bar, people, and jurors. He had a great faculty for remembering faces and names, and could call a man by name and locate him if he had once served as a juror in his court. Our relations were always pleasant. But Judge Humphrey had political aspirations and was elected a member of Congress in 1876, in which capacity he served three terms. He succeeded Jeremiah M. Rusk, who also had served three terms, which seem to have been silently agreed upon as the length of service in Congress in that district.

In January, 1877, a bar convention met at Baldwin to name a candidate to succeed Judge Humphrey. Many candidates were suggested: H. C. Baker of Hudson, S. J.

White of Prescott, Bundy of Menomonie, Bailey of Eau Claire, and Clough also of Hudson and formerly, when residing at Superior, judge of the Eleventh Circuit. It was a harmonious gathering in spite of the numerous candidates, and resulted in the nomination of Mr. Bundy. Bundy was well known as a Democrat, and the district being overwhelmingly Republican it was not surprising that the cry should go out that the judge ought to be a Republican. H. E. Houghton of Durand, who was in every way a capable and respectable attorney, but who had not participated in the convention, listened to the tempting call and announced himself a candidate. It was naturally claimed that the people and not the bar should have the naming of the judge. This was alluring; but what are attorneys save agents of clients? And who are better qualified to judge of the qualifications for the judgeship? I took an active part in the campaign for Mr. Bundy, having been a supporter in his nomination. The bar generally stood by him, and his election by a large majority emphasized the view that judicial officers should not be chosen on partisan lines—a practice which has prevailed in Wisconsin.

Judge Bundy served the circuit for many years, and made an admirable and impartial judge. He continued a Democrat, but that certainly did not show itself on the bench. I continued as reporter, and we formed a close and permanent friendship. That he had the kindest feeling towards me he evidenced in my later political life. I have every reason for believing that he always voted for me, probably the only exception he made in the ticket. While I was a member of Congress and he was still on the bench, he once wrote me that he was anxious to improve his financial condition and proposed that he resign or not stand for reëlection, and that we form a partnership in the law practice at

the end of my then term. He served as judge nineteen years.
Relations between him and Mr. Houghton remained pleasant and cordial as formerly. Houghton served in the state
senate, and later removed to Spokane, Washington, where
he died.

Among the members of the bar during my service in
court, many men of ability and eminence appeared. But as
a keen lawyer, forgetting himself in the interest of his client,
diligent and fearless, I do not think there was anyone in the
state who excelled John C. Spooner before he entered politics and when he devoted himself exclusively to his practice.
I have seen him appear against former Chief Justice Dixon,
William F. Vilas, Senator Davis of St. Paul, and other attorneys of the very highest standing, and he always held his
own; he knew his case, was ready with authorities, and never
surprised. Judge Dixon was at one time defending the city
of Hudson in a personal injury case and was somewhat an-
noyed when Spooner sprung some of his own decisions on
him as to the admission of evidence. In that case, in tran-
scribing the evidence I wrote "black" fracture instead of
"oblique" fracture. Colonel Spooner called my attention to
it—the only mistake, so far as I recollect, called to my attention during my service as reporter. But the outline "blk"
was the same for both words, according to Graham. It has
been stated by observers that after serving as Senator,
Spooner showed in court a self-consciousness which had not
appeared in his earlier career at the bar. He evidently felt
that the public was watching him and, perhaps uncon-
sciously, did not forget the "galleries." He was a ready
and effective speaker at the bar and before the public.

POLITICAL LIFE

I had at this time no intention of entering politics, or ambition to do so. I did intend, as soon as my economic condi-

tion warranted, to resign as court reporter (as I did later)
and devote myself to the practice of law. It was a surprise
to me when Dr. A. D. Andrews, then state senator, a leading
and, I may say, *the* leading citizen of River Falls, said to
me one day in the approaching campaign of 1878: "Haugen,
we are going to nominate you for the assembly." I replied,
"Doctor, I do not want it, and can't afford to give up my reporting to go to the assembly. It would interfere with my
work." I also said that I would not spend one cent to secure
a nomination. He replied that that would not be necessary;
that the session of the legislature would come at a time when
there were very few sessions of court, and that there would
be no difficulty to secure leave of absence to attend them.
The interview was ended by his requesting me to attend the
county convention. This I did, and was nominated without
any effort on my part. During the day some friends, candidates for county offices, came to me and urged me to see
some of the delegates, "or we will all be defeated." I said to
them, "I am not a candidate, and they need not nominate
me if they don't want to." I was more ambitious to become
a fairly good lawyer than a mediocre politician. A session
or two in the legislature is not, however, to be considered as
lost time to a young attorney. It gives him an inside view
of legislation not to be spurned. The county was strongly
Republican, and a nomination was equivalent to an election.
I had naturally as reporter acquired a large acquaintance in
the county, where I had lived from the time I was six years
old. It had become somewhat a custom to give a man two
terms in the legislature, so I was nominated and elected the
next year as a matter of course. I was followed by my good
friend and later partner, Franklin L. Gilson, who also
served two years, the latter as speaker.

The service in the assembly was pleasant and agreeable, and not nearly so strenuous as reporting. There was a mutual good-fellowship regardless of partisanship or of that factional feeling of late apparently prevalent. I served on the committees of education and judiciary. The legislative houses were open to outsiders, and anyone could enter at any time. The members did not fear their own corruption and seek protection for their own honesty behind closed doors. David M. Kelly of Green Bay was the speaker during my first year in the assembly and was a model presiding officer, very precise and accurate in putting the questions before the house. Among the members were William E. Carter of Grant County, once nominated for attorney general and declining the nomination; John Brindley, also of Grant and for many years until his recent death county judge of La Crosse County; Joseph V. Quarles, later United States Senator; Atley Peterson, my successor as railroad commissioner in 1887, the heavyweight of the assembly; Richard J. Burdge of Rock, George G. Cox of Iowa, and many others; now all gone, but good, reliable public servants and personal friends. As I look back on the membership in 1879 and 1880, old Father Time seems to have taken them all; I know of no one now living, although there may be.

The first year of my service the legislature adjourned about the last of March, and the second year the very early days of April; in fact, nearly all the members went home before the spring election and did not return. But the session was continuous while it lasted, evening sessions being general. The state was in a stage of development; much special legislation was sought and considered. Besides, we had in 1879 a long and bitter contest over the election of a United States Senator. Matthew H. Carpenter had served in that capacity with distinction to himself and to the state, but had been defeated in 1875 for a second term. His defeat was generally attributed to the fact that he had voted for an increase in the pay of Senators and Representatives from five thousand dollars a year to seven thousand five hundred dollars, the act to take effect immediately upon its passage—the so-called "back-pay steal" in the campaign of 1874. He had been nominated by the Republican members of the legislature in 1875, but a few members of the party bolted the nomination fairly won according to political usage and methods, and joined the Democratic members, with the result that Angus Cameron of La Crosse, a Republican, was elected as a compromise. The final election of Cameron by a majority of Democrats was generally credited to his Democratic partner, Joseph W. Losey, an able attorney and a leader in the Democratic party. What would our present self-styled Progressives answer to the charge that they have twice assisted in increasing their salary, first by fifty per cent and finally doubling it so that it is now ten thousand dollars a year, not even daring to go on record for their conviction, if such they had, but quietly favoring the "steal," as it was called in 1874? And what would be the popular vote on the subject, if submitted? Senator Carpenter voted openly and defended his action. Judging by the present defeat at the polls of the proposed increase of the pay of members of the legislature, which was certainly modest compared with the increase voted themselves by members of Congress, the only safe thing is the absolute silence observed by the latter, while they are bewailing the distress of the farmer, who is helpless as to his income and is taxed to pay their increased salaries.

The announced candidates for the senatorship in 1875 were Senator Carpenter, Senator Timothy O. Howe, standing for reëlection, and E. W. Keyes of Madison. Mr. Keyes had for many years been chairman of the Republican state

central committee and was quite generally known as "Boss
Keyes." My early partner and editor, Mr. Morse, always
referred to him by that title. He had been a force within the
party and a generous distributor of patronage. During the
preëlection campaign nothing was said, at least not in
Pierce County, as to my preference on the senatorship.
Coming out of the courthouse at Hudson one day, Colonel
Spooner asked me how I felt on the question. I said that I
was entirely uncommitted, but I felt that Carpenter had not
been fairly treated four years before and was inclined to
support him. Mr. Spooner certainly did not disagree with
that sentiment at the time, but later during the contest he
threw his influence to Keyes. He was the active attorney of
the Omaha—then known as the West Wisconsin—Railway
Company, not only in court proceedings but also before the
legislature. Keyes was also a lobbyist, or representative,
of railroads during legislative sessions, so it may be readily
seen why the two had to work in harmony. The Omaha
had a land grant and other interests that must be taken
care of, and Spooner was as active and efficient before
the legislature as he was before the courts. As far as my
observation went, nothing was done by either that would
justify criticism, and I am not using the term "lobbyist" in
any objectionable sense. I do not recollect that Spooner
approached me on the subject of the senatorship at Madison,
although I suspected that Keyes had been assured through
another source that when the time came he could rely on my
vote. Senator Andrews was in the same position as myself,
and we both voted from beginning to end in the caucuses
for Carpenter. Twenty-five members became known as the
"True to Matt" group, and I have a picture of them sent
by Carpenter friends in commemoration of the struggle,
which lasted, by caucusing every evening, for more than a

week and resulted in the nomination and election of our
candidate. At the beginning the vote was rather evenly divided. Keyes was not known as an ardent reformer, and the
"back-pay steal" battle cry could not be very effective in his
behalf. Later he became involved in another three-cornered
contest for the nomination for Congress, which resulted in
the first nomination of Robert M. La Follette to that position. While unsuccessful when himself a candidate, Keyes
was a power within the party and seemed to enjoy the game.
He did not seem to harbor any lasting rancor when the fight
was over, but stood by the party nominee loyally. Matt Carpenter died before his term expired. He was beyond question the most brilliant orator that Wisconsin has sent to
either house of Congress, a leader at the bar at an early date,
and one of the attorneys in the Barstow-Bashford contest
for the governorship in 1856. In his *Life of Carpenter,*
Frank Flower states that Carpenter withdrew from the case
when it became apparent that his client's claim to the office
was based on false returns from a couple of election districts
in Dunn and Polk counties.

Charles L. Colby was a member of the assembly from
Milwaukee in 1880. He was one of the two trustees of the
Wisconsin Central Railroad, which had recently extended
its road to Ashland, being aided in the enterprise by a liberal
land grant, the lands thus given it having by legislation been
exempted from taxation for ten years. The period of exemption expiring, Mr. Colby quite naturally asked that it
be extended; this was probably one of his main purposes in
coming to the legislature. The vote was close in the assembly, and the extension of the exemption was defeated by
one vote on motion to reconsider, having passed by one vote
the preceding day. It was creditable to the membership that
the lines held so true, the motion to reconsider having been

made and defeated by a motion to adjourn. Mr. Colby was
a ready debater and must be ranked with the leaders of the
assembly in ability. I believe this was the last attempt to
secure exemption from taxation of railroads in Wisconsin.
The Wisconsin Central has never ranked with the better-
paying roads of the state. Traffic does not move north and
south; and, while there followed great developments in the
mining region tributary to it, the haul was short and sea-
sonal. In extending its line to St. Paul it met the rivalry
of roads well established as to traffic.

William E. Smith was governor, Hans B. Warner secretary of state, and Richard Guenther state treasurer during
my legislative service. After the Civil War paper money—
and there was no other—was at a discount, falling at one
time below fifty per cent. Deflation was slow. No metal
money in circulation. Small change was "shinplaster." I
think it was in 1873 that President Grant in his message ad-
vising the return to the gold basis said: "The way to resume
is to resume." The Resumption Act was passed, but did not
provide for going into full effect until January, 1879. Mr.
Guenther, the state treasurer, had provided himself with
gold currency to celebrate the event by paying the members
of the legislature, or at least offering to do so, in gold on
their assembling in January that year. But knowing that
we could have gold, paper was as a rule preferred. The pay
at the time was three hundred and fifty dollars per annum.
After the passage of the Resumption Act in 1873 the paper
money began to rise and reached par some time before 1879.
The inflation at that time had been an inflation of the value
of gold, while the inflation following the World War seems
to have been that of property, and may be slower and more
difficult of adjustment, whether economically or by legisla-

tion. Doctors and quacks are proposing remedies, with the race at present seemingly in favor of the quacks.

Hans B. Warner of Pierce County had been elected secretary of state in 1877 and was serving his second term. Two terms were something of an established rule. To pass the honors around was the method of caucuses and conventions. Perhaps it kept government and officials in closer touch with and more responsive to the public demand.

Except for the senatorial election in 1879 there was no particular excitement during either session of my service. Perhaps I should mention, however, the so-called Oshkosh steam wagon. In 1875 the legislature had passed an act offering a bonus of ten thousand dollars for the invention and construction of a steam motor that would be a practical substitute for horse power on the highway and on the farm. A wagon was constructed at Oshkosh and was driven by its own power to Madison during the winter of 1879, the owner thereupon claiming the award. My recollection is that it took the machine some three or four days to make the trip from Oshkosh. It was on exhibition for the benefit of the legislators, and I had a ride in it around the Capitol Park and perhaps out State Street. It was a slow-moving affair, and it was quite evident that while it did operate its own weight it was not a substitute for horse power. William Wall, a member of the legislature from Oshkosh, had introduced the bill and worked faithfully to secure its passage. A compromise was finally arrived at and the inventor was paid five thousand dollars.

Another incident of note—I think in the session of 1880— was the stringing of a wire from the Capitol to the University, over which wire people were able to talk to one another. This was the first telephone in Madison. Ladies—among them my wife—tried the instrument, and they would turn and giggle and laugh when they heard the voice at the other end.

Lobbyists were always on hand at the legislative sessions, but the danger of corruption was not even suggested. During my nearly thirty years of public service I cannot point to a single instance where I thought a public official was corruptly influenced. He may have been unduly influenced and swayed, but I have never thought "bought," as is often charged.

Franklin L. Gilson followed me in the assembly. He was a brother of Judge N. S. Gilson, circuit judge of the Fond du Lac circuit and later for many years chairman of the State Tax Commission during my membership in that body. I had continued to serve as court reporter, but never abandoned the idea of following the profession of law, for which I had prepared. The duties of reporter were also in the line of that preparation. The circuit had been changed during the years. Judge Henry D. Barron had become judge of the upper district, taking in Chippewa, Barron, and Polk on the south. I served with him a couple of years in addition to serving in the Eighth. Barron had been in politics for many years, but could not be said to hold a prominent position at the bar. He had served in the assembly eight years, had been a state senator, and had held one of the auditorships of the Treasury Department at Washington for a time; he was speaker of the assembly during his last years in that body. He was an all-round politician and kept up his political interests after going on the bench. Through him I first became interested in the State Historical Society, of which he was a life member. I resigned my position in his court about 1879. After the election of Mr. Gilson to the assembly in 1880 he and I agreed to go into partnership, he to move to River Falls when he re-

turned from Madison. This plan was carried out, and I sent
my resignation to Judge Bundy, receiving from him a very
friendly and appreciative letter in reply, expressing regret
at the breaking off of our close relationship of several years'
standing. Judge Bundy was a man of sterling integrity,
well versed in the law. He was not of the oratorical style,
but rather hesitating in his speech, sometimes "back-stitch-
ing," as stenographers would say. On one occasion I had
taken in shorthand his charge to the jury, and the attorney
for the losing party was making a motion for a new trial,
basing it in part on the charge. He read a part of the charge
which the judge did not recognize, when I asked to be al-
lowed to read it. I read it as the judge had given it, and he
said, "Yes, that is the way I said it, but that is different
from the way you [the attorney] read it."

HANS B. WARNER

Hans B. Warner had been county clerk of Pierce County
for many years before he became secretary of state. His
family came to the town of Martell a few weeks later than
my father, and took up land in the hardwood belt. His
father was Peder Peterson, and the rest of the children went
by the name of Peterson. Hans became a member of the
family of Judson Warner, an American, and after quite a
number of years—in fact, after serving in the army—was
legally adopted by Warner, thus becoming legally entitled
to the name under which he had enlisted. He was a good-na-
tured and popular official, but with only a meager common-
school education. He became to some extent at least a political protegé of Mr. Keyes, and was encouraged to become a
candidate for governor in 1881. Mr. Keyes was no doubt
anxious to reëstablish himself after his defeat for the senatorship in 1879, and here was Mr. Warner, an ex-soldier,

wounded in the war, a Scandinavian by birth, and a popular official. But there was another ex-soldier in the field: Jeremiah M. Rusk of Vernon County, who had served three terms in Congress. As to education, the two ranked somewhat alike. Rusk was a robust old fellow, with an abundance of common sense, whole-hearted and sincere. There was no blot on the escutcheon of either; both were men of good character. It was the age of the veteran in politics. Pierce County was naturally for Warner, and Mr. Gilson and I were both sent as delegates to the state convention at Madison on September 20. On reaching Elroy the evening before, we received the information that President Garfield had died that day, the nineteenth. Both Mr. Gilson and I had attended the national convention at Chicago in 1880 when Garfield was nominated after a week of contention between the three hundred and five solid phalanx for Grant and the bitter opposition led by Blaine forces. I have preserved in my diary a record of each vote as taken, and it shows that thirty-six ballots were taken before a nomination was reached.

But to return to the state convention in 1881. Mr. Warner showed considerable strength, but the forces of General Rusk were massed and solid, and resulted in his nomination after several ballots. It had become a matter of political policy to recognize different nationalities in making up the ticket. Mr. Warner had probably mainly for that reason been placed on the ticket when first nominated. He was now defeated. There were aspirants for recognition, among them our old friend Halle Steensland of Madison for state treasurer. During an intermission in the meeting William E. Carter of Grant, with whom I had served in the assembly, came to me and said that they would nominate me for railroad commissioner, that office having been made elective during the preceding session of the legislature. As my name had not been mentioned by anyone or anywhere, so far as I knew, for any state office, the suggestion came as a surprise. I told Mr. Carter that I was not a candidate and could not answer him until I had talked over the matter with Mr. Warner. This I did, together with Mr. Gilson. Hans Warner was a good fellow and said, as he naturally would, that even though he had been defeated for the nomination for governor, there was no reason why I should decline the nomination for the office suggested. The nomination of Edward McFetridge for treasurer and Ernst Timme for secretary of state had left the office of railroad commissioner open. The upshot of it was that I was nominated without any previous effort on my part, in somewhat the same manner as my first nomination for the assembly. My support of Senator Carpenter in 1879 undoubtedly contributed mainly in giving me the nomination. Mr. Warner had had the support of Mr. Keyes and friends in seeking the governorship; but the party management had gone out of Madison with the defeat of Keyes, and the headquarters of the central committee had gone to Milwaukee, with Edward Sanderson as chairman and Henry C. Payne as secretary, the latter remaining in active management of party affairs for many years. The ticket was made up as follows: for governor, Jeremiah M. Rusk of Vernon; lieutenant governor, Sam S. Fifield of Ashland; secretary of state, Ernst G. Timme of Kenosha; treasurer, Edward McFetridge of Dodge; attorney general, Leander F. Frisby of Washington; state superintendent, Robert Graham of Winnebago; railroad commissioner, Nils P. Haugen of Pierce; insurance commissioner, Philip Spooner of Dane. All were elected, and we formed a harmonious official family, working well together for the general and not merely party welfare. Governor

Rusk was a heroic figure physically and of good metal mentally. His lack of education was more than compensated for by his sterling good common sense and courage to take responsibility when occasion demanded. Timme had served in the Sixth Wisconsin and had lost a hand. His predecessor, Warner, had also been wounded in the hand in service and had lost the forefinger.

I could not claim any particular qualification for the office to which I was elected, but I studied the statutes and also the reports of my predecessors and of railroad commissions of other states. The report of the Massachusetts commission was particularly instructive, more so than any other. Charles Francis Adams, Jr., as chairman of that commission, had made a thorough study of the control of public transportation in this country and had visited Europe for further information, and his report was comprehensive and educational, especially to a novice.

The Wisconsin commission consisted of the commissioner and a secretary. James H. Foster of Winnebago had served in the latter capacity under my predecessor, Jack Turner of Portage, and during the convention had loyally supported his chief for the nomination. It was no doubt a surprise to him when he received my letter asking him to continue his service with me. I had had plenty of applications, but thought best to have someone in the office with some knowledge of what had gone on before. The commissioner was not clad with much authority. He made investigations upon receiving complaints, and if his advice was ignored by the railroad he made report to the attorney general, who was then directed to prosecute on behalf of the complainant. The office, created during the Granger excitement following 1873, was at first composed of three members, but was later reduced to one commissioner. Complaints were not infre-

quent. As to passenger and freight charges, I do not recollect reporting a single one to the attorney general. They
were all settled, and I suspect in less important matters by
giving the complainant some special favor, like an annual
pass for himself and family. A complaint of overcharge between Milwaukee and Madison I took up first with the general freight office in Milwaukee, but was, I thought, somewhat curtly treated by the official in charge. A law had been
passed limiting freight rates in the state so as not to exceed
those in effect in 1873. The rate in question being in clear
violation of that statute, I immediately went to the office of
Roswell Miller, then general manager of the St. Paul road,
who without hesitation called the freight czar on the carpet
and told him to readjust the rate and settle with the complainant. A more important question arose as to rates from
Chicago to Oshkosh. The roads serving that point and also
Green Bay were in the habit of charging a higher rate to
Oshkosh from Chicago than through that city to Green Bay,
where they met with lake competition. I took up the matter
with the companies, without satisfactory results, and appointed a hearing at Oshkosh. The roads evidently did not
want that question brought into the limelight; for on the
morning set for the hearing one of the railroad officials came
to Madison with a written statement from the complainants
that the matter had been settled and the complaints withdrawn. The same thing occurred with reference to grain
rates from points in Grant County. What the terms of settlement were I never learned. These are only sample in-
stances.

The roads avoided open hearings or court trials and made
their settlements privately. An instance occurred on the
Omaha road near the station of Richardson in Polk County.
A farmer complained that the road recently constructed

through his farm did not have the necessary culverts and that backwater drowned out his meadow. Going up over the road with some of the officials of the company, I asked them why they could not remedy the matter by providing the necessary outlet. They said they could and would. A few years later when I met one of the officers, he reminded me of the matter and stated that they had followed my suggestion, but that later the same man had sued the company for setting fire to and burning up his meadow. So in some cases the railroads caught it going and coming.

While these notes have been in preparation, Marvin Hughitt, for many years a leader among presidents and managers of railroads of the Northwest, has passed away. I had occasion to meet him a number of times while serving as railroad commissioner, and found him a gentleman in every respect, a nobleman in the truer sense of that term. To mention one occasion: I was invited to accompany a delegation from Ellsworth to interview Mr. Hughitt with reference to the location of a station at that place, to which the road was then being extended from Hudson. Mr. Hughitt was the president of the Omaha Railway Company. We had our meeting and when the matter was presented Mr. Hughitt courteously told the delegates that he would place a station wherever they desired—in the village, which is on a somewhat high plateau, or at East Ellsworth, which is much lower. The delegation chose East Ellsworth, and I believe made a mistake which has since been regretted. But the station was located according to their wishes. Mr. Hughitt received with the utmost courtesy any complaint made. He was always referred to by his subordinates with characteristic friendliness and devotion. While a member of the Tax Commission many years later, when railroad assessments were under consideration, Frank Crandon, tax commissioner of the Northwestern Railway Company, himself an old man, after arguments before the commission used to say to us, "What can I tell Mr. Hughitt?" Mr. Hughitt was the father of the official family.

Passes in those days were distributed freely to members of the legislature, state officers, and other men of influence, or supposed influence, on public sentiment. Governor Rusk refused to accept the usual form of free pass. He insisted that as the executive of the state he was entitled to free passage as a matter of right and not as a favor. The railroads complied with his request and gave him a letter instructing all conductors to pass Governor Rusk. I was entitled to the same privilege, as the law expressly provided for the free passage of the railroad commissioner; but I took the general pass. The pass question became a nuisance, and requests came to me from persons I did not know, asking for passes. In special cases I asked for them, and was never refused. I had never had a pass until I was elected to the legislature. The judges I served with had them, and presumably I might have had them on application through proper channels. After I was elected to Congress in January, 1887, I returned with courteous acknowledgment all passes sent me, feeling that while given only in friendly spirit according to long-established custom, the legislator, like Caesar's wife, ought to keep himself beyond criticism as to undue influence. I believe I was the only member of Congress from Wisconsin who did not at that time accept passes; but to me the matter had become a nuisance, as it undoubtedly was to the leading railway officials. It was later under the leadership of Assemblyman A. R. Hall of Dunn County that public sentiment was aroused on the subject, resulting in legislation depriving public officials of the privilege.

The part of the Omaha Railway known at the time as
the North Wisconsin was extending its line to Superior
and Bayfield, and Governor Rusk appointed me to examine
the extensions and certify to him the facts, as the completion
of each twenty miles entitled the company to a certain acreage under the land grant accorded it. I made several trips
for that purpose over the new line together with officials of
the company. In reporting to the governor, my certification
stated that the necessary mileage had been constructed with
"all necessary sidings, switches, stations, depots," etc., following the language of the land grant law. Governor Rusk
looked up at me and said: "I don't believe they have done all
that." I replied that my certificate said "all necessary,"
and he said, "Well, that is the lawyer of it." When the road
was built the cedar and tamarack marshes along the right
of way presented an almost solid wall of timber or trees on
each side. But with dead tops and branches left from the
clearing, fires quickly followed and the magnificent sight of
this luxuriant forest disappeared forever. While the forest
was untouched by man, fires ran through it and lapped up
the leaves without doing serious damage to the trees. This
had been and was the case in Pierce County even after its
settlement. The settlers in clearing land took care of the
debris. But when the lumbermen left the slashings, fires resulted in holocausts like those of Peshtigo and later at
Hinckley, Minnesota, destroying every green tree for miles.

My term and the service connected with it was on the
whole pleasant; the railroad officials were courteous and I
formed relations about the state that stood me in good stead
later; that is, from a political standpoint. I kept up a nominal partnership with Mr. Gilson, and Charles Smith was
later taken into the firm; both genial and agreeable comrades. I had necessarily been interrupted in the practice of

law, first as court reporter and later by getting into state politics, but had even when not in partnership with others to some extent continued a small practice when consistent with my reporting in court. The reporting itself was a pretty good education, at least as to rules of evidence and practice in court. I have been fairly successful in public life. Still I would say to any young attorney ambitious to succeed, let politics alone; stick to your law. There are more pitfalls in politics than in private practice of the profession; many more disappointed lives. Even in the most successful years of my political life I looked forward to a time spent in the practice, and in the enjoyment of private life. Politics never had the allurement for me that it seems to have for many. However, I did enjoy the personal associations and friendships formed.

While railroad commissioner I recommended in one of the annual reports the adoption of Central Time for the state, and drew a bill to that effect, which was passed. Before that, trains running between Chicago and St. Paul made a change in time of twenty minutes at Elroy. I also had the first railroad map of the state made and published. Mr. Foster was a faithful and efficient assistant in preparing the reports, and I had no reason to regret having appointed him. It was in harmony with my ideas of the best civil service, before there was any civil service law in the state. The larger railroads were paying a license fee of four per cent on their gross earnings in the state in lieu of taxes; the smaller roads at a lower rate. The sleeping-car companies had not been included and escaped taxation. I recommended that they be subjected to the same license fee as the larger roads, and helped to prepare a bill for that purpose. The representatives of the companies, however, caused the bill to be so amended as to read "earnings made between points within the state," or words to that effect; the result being the exemption of any part of the earnings where the travel was interstate. To illustrate, a person desiring to purchase a ticket from Madison to Hudson was given a ticket from Madison to St. Paul; or, from Madison to Superior the sleeping-car ticket would read to Duluth, thus making the trip interstate. The very object of the bill was thus frustrated.

During this period a constitutional amendment was adopted changing state elections from the odd-numbered years to the even-numbered, to correspond with federal elections, and the terms of the then state officers had been extended for a year to correspond. All having been reëlected, we thus served five years instead of four.

WILLIAM T. PRICE

William T. Price had for some years aspired to congressional honors. He was a man of energy and enterprise, residing at Black River Falls, and had acquired some money and property in the lumber business on Black River. He was a logger, not a manufacturer of lumber. He was a member of the state senate in 1879 and 1880, a ready and fluent speaker, and one of the earliest radical prohibitionists in the state. He had been a candidate for the congressional nomination against General Rusk, and an enmity had grown up between the two which had lasted for years. Mr. Price was a candidate for the nomination in 1882, and some of Governor Rusk's friends had their knives out for him. One charge against Price was that he had been cutting pine on government lands. I remember being present in the federal court at Madison some time before the campaign of 1882 got well under way, when the calendar for the term was called. There was a case of the government against Price. The attorney for the government for some reason wanted the case to go over the term, when Bill Price, not leaving the matter to his attorney, sprang to his feet and shouted, "I don't want this case to go over; I want this matter settled now. I intend to be a candidate for Congress next summer, and I don't want this thing to hang over me." My impression is that the case never came to trial; it was probably discontinued. The occurrence was Price all over. But cutting over the line by lumbermen was not uncommon in early days. An old Norwegian settler in Pierce County came into my office in River Falls once and asked advice, saying that he was threatened with a lawsuit for cutting timber on speculator lands adjoining his own. The term "speculator" was common when land was owned by a nonresident. He said that he had cut over the line some, but he had done so because when he first came to the country he worked for Jake Lord in the pineries and Jake told his men that they could cut over the line as far as they could throw the ax. Jake Lord was a fine old fellow of the pioneer type living in River Falls. I joshed him about it; he just laughed; nothing more. If Price "cut over the line," he no doubt had plenty of precedents. He had a sharp tongue, and it is likely that the old feud was more his fault than Rusk's. But in the campaign of 1882 I became somewhat of a go-between, being a friend of both and in favor of Price for the nomination. Price called on me in Madison and asked me to go with him into some parts of the district where I was best acquainted. I said that he must call on the Governor, that he would find Rusk friendly if approached. The result was that we went into the Governor's office. They had a social chat and the old feeling was evidently at an end. Price was elected and reëlected twice, and made a creditable record. He was a true and tried Republican. He was entirely independent, although adhering to party lines on what were considered essential party questions. People said he was "profane," but

Bill Price indignantly denied this, saying that the language he used was for emphasis and the best at his command, and that it was not profanity.

The nominating convention of 1886 was approaching, and I had determined—or "chosen"—not to be a candidate for another term, intending to reënter the law firm at River Falls with which I had maintained a quasi connection. Governor Rusk and Secretary of State Timme were renominated at the convention; both were veterans of the Civil War. Rusk had taken a decided stand in the labor riots at Milwaukee, and it was thought that his conduct required the approval of the party, as it had caused some criticism in the opposition press. It will be recollected that a company of the state militia in Milwaukee had been called out to suppress a riot and on the threatening approach of the mob the captain had ordered "Fire!" and, if I remember correctly, five men had been killed or wounded. It may be doubted whether Rusk was directly responsible for the firing. The captain may have acted hastily. But the rioting ended, and Rusk assumed the responsibility manfully. When complimented on his action on his return to Madison, he was reported in the press to have replied: "I seen my duty and I done it"; truly Rusk. I met the Governor in the lobby of the Plankinton House, Milwaukee, early on the morning after the shooting, and he told me about it. A Democratic newspaperman called him to one side. They had a short conversation, after which the Governor returned to his seat and said, "Mr. ⸺ says I did the right thing and he will stand by me." But the paper represented did not stand by him; evidently it thought it a party advantage to attack him for "shooting workingmen." Throughout the state his action met with approval, and he was reëlected by a large majority.

CHAPTER III

CAREER IN CONGRESS

My term as railroad commissioner being about to expire, I intended to resume the practice of law and had an understanding with Frank Ross, a practicing attorney of Prescott and district attorney of Pierce County, with a view of entering into partnership with him and moving to the then promising city of West Superior.

William T. Price died after a short illness on the first Monday in December, 1886, the very day of the reassembling of the Forty-ninth Congress for its short session. All the state officers attended the funeral at Black River Falls. The Northwestern and Omaha railroads placed a special train at the disposal of the governor and other officials in honor of Mr. Price's memory. We had entered the car in the evening to return to Madison, when Governor Rusk came to me and said: "Step outside; some men want to see you." Quite a number who had no doubt come to attend the funeral met me, and one of them acting as spokesman said that they had talked over the matter and had concluded to ask me to become a candidate for the term in Congress to which Mr. Price had been reëlected the previous month. It was a surprise, and I said I should have to consider the matter; that possibly Mr. Warner from my own county might be a candidate, in which event it would not be wise for both to run; that I must find out first what his intentions might be. As I was foot-free again, the suggestion coming as it did was flattering, to say the least. Governor Rusk heartily encouraged my candidacy. After a few days in Madison I went to Ellsworth, the home of Mr. Warner, and had an interview with him and with friends of both of us. He assured me he had no intention of being a candidate, and I was encouraged to try it out, although I knew by that time that Joseph G. Thorpe, a wealthy lumberman of Eau Claire, who had been defeated for the position in previous conventions, had already announced himself. The district consisted of fifteen counties, embracing Trempealeau, Jackson, and Clark on the south and east, and reaching to Lake Superior on the north, including Douglas and Bayfield, but not Ashland. It had according to the census of 1890 over two hundred and fifty thousand inhabitants. On this occasion I made a campaign for the nomination. The lumber interests had to quite an extent domineered in politics, and Thorpe was a prominent representative of those interests.

Governor Rusk ordered a special election to be held January 18, 1887, and the congressional convention was called to meet January 7 at Eau Claire. The convention met in due time and all the counties were represented. There were several "favorite sons" supported by their county delegates: Senator Noah D. Comstock of Trempealeau, August Finkelnburg of Buffalo, and others. Horace A. Taylor, then chairman of the Republican state central committee, had aspirations, but he came to the convention as a delegate from St. Croix County instructed for me, and he obeyed instructions—I fear, somewhat reluctantly. There was reason for believing that after a few ballots the local candidates would withdraw and at least some of those counties would come to me. That was especially true of Trempealeau, Buffalo, and Dunn. The last-named had voted for Rockwell J. Flint, always a good and firm friend, then and now. I led from the start, and when a recess was taken for supper I had thirty-nine votes; necessary to nominate, forty-three. I think I remember the figures correctly. I lacked four votes. I approached Mr. Comstock, who had the support of his delegates from Trempealeau County, and asked him if he expected to be nominated; I said that if he did I would not ask him to withdraw. He replied that he did not expect to be nominated and would withdraw and when the meeting reconvened ask his delegates to vote for me, but we would not give the matter out. On my way to the hotel Mr. Taylor joined me and said: "Haugen, you cannot be nominated and you had better withdraw." I replied that being the leading candidate I should never be able to explain my withdrawal to my friends; that I had better be defeated in the convention; but I added: "I am going to be nominated on the next ballot." At this he poo-poohed with the air of a superior knowledge of politics. Hugh H. Price, son of William Price, had announced himself a candidate to succeed his father, and had an instructed delegation from his county. As some of them were the very men who had first approached me on the subject, I felt free to suggest to them that Mr. Price be given the short term to expire with the short session of the sitting Congress, and that I would suggest that course of action to other supporters. To this they readily agreed. On the first ballot after the recess, and after the nomination of Mr. Price for the short term, I had an even larger majority than I had expected. Thus I defeated Mr. Thorpe, a representative lumberman, a man of wealth and the father-in-law of Ole Bull, the Norwegian violinist, and Mr. Taylor all in one set-to.

But the campaign was on, and the Democrats nominated as my opponent Doctor Johnson, one of the leading physicians of the state and president then or shortly thereafter of the State Medical Society. He was also the local physician and surgeon of the Omaha Railroad, an able and highly respectable candidate, and a personal friend then and later.

He resided in Hudson, the home of Mr. Taylor. It was related that engines were run during election day to carry the railroad workers to the polls, undoubtedly largely through friendship for Doctor Johnson. The Eau Claire lumbermen seemed also to have deserted me, and that county gave something like twelve hundred majority for Johnson. In spite of this I carried the district by something like thirteen hundred majority. Knowing of the disaffection in Eau Claire and in part at least in Hudson, I wrote Mr. Taylor during the campaign that as chairman of the Republican state central committee I had a right to ask his active support. His answer was that the state central committee had nothing to do with congressional elections. This I stored up in my memory for later use. That he had been itching for the nomination himself at the convention, expecting it to come as the result of a deadlock, I have no doubt. He probably depended on his position as the head of the party in the state to assist him, but his county had instructed for me, and there were men in the delegation, among them my friend Hans Borchsenius of Baldwin, keeping close watch of the trend of affairs. It had been a custom of candidates for state office to contribute ten per cent of one year's salary to the campaign fund, to be disposed of by the central committee, which amount I had contributed in former campaigns. When in 1888 I was a candidate for reëlection to Congress, I received notice from the committee, Mr. Taylor being chairman and Henry Payne of Milwaukee secretary, that I had been assessed five hundred dollars as my share of the campaign fund. I answered saying that in my former campaign the chairman had informed me that the state central committee had nothing to do with congressional campaigns, and that I would, as he had left me to do then, conduct my campaign independently of the state central committee. I never contributed to the committee in any of my succeeding cam-

paigns, nor did any of them cost me five hundred dollars.
That of the special election cost me over two thousand dollars, partly due to the fact that in many localities the candidates had to pay for the printing of tickets, and at that particular election I was considered about the only Republican
candidate. There was no official ballot until some years
later.

SPOONER AND TAYLOR

In addition to his prominence as an attorney, John C.
Spooner was one of the leading Republicans of the state and
admittedly one of the best stump speakers. His recognized
ability naturally suggested him as a proper candidate for the
position of United States senator. He was the attorney of
a railroad company, it is true, but the feeling against railroads had abated somewhat after the Granger excitement
commencing with the election of Governor William R. Taylor in 1873. Spooner and Hod Taylor were neighbors in
Hudson. Taylor was a newspaper man; a man of considerable ability, a good public speaker, and an adroit politician;
and had, as stated above, ambitions. He had served under
President Hayes as consul at Marseilles during that Republican administration. Spooner before removing to Hudson
had served as private secretary to Governor Fairchild. He
had also served in the army during the Civil War. Taylor
had no army record. Spooner became an avowed candidate
for the senatorship in the election of 1884, and was recognized
as such during the campaign, in which he actively engaged.
During the fall—it may have been after the election—
he accosted me on the street in Hudson and asked me to come
up to his office. He asked me what he ought to do when
friends advised him that he could not be nominated and
elected by the legislature to convene in January. I naturally

wanted to know what friend had so advised him, and he said Hod Taylor. I answered him in about these words: "You have taken an active part in the campaign, everybody understanding that you would be a candidate, and you cannot well withdraw now; besides, I think you will be elected." He had had correspondence with many of the legislators-elect and had received encouragement. Either then, or later, he asked me to go to Arcadia in Trempealeau County and see Senator Comstock for him; said he had written him, but received no answer. I suggested that as Mr. Comstock was a much older man than I, I hesitated to interview him, but I would do so if he would get Professor Thayer, then of the River Falls Normal School faculty, to go with me. Professor Thayer was institute conductor and well known throughout the state. We met by appointment in Winona and wired Mr. Comstock that we would be in Arcadia on the next train. He evidently did not like the idea of two politicians running after him, and met us at the train, got aboard, and went with us to Merrillan. Being told our errand, he said: "What is the matter with Spooner anyway? I have written him that I am for him, but I am not publishing it abroad." When the legislature convened the friends of Spooner met for consultation, Comstock not present. He had a room near the Park Hotel. Spooner again asked me to interview him, stating that he had not had a word from him. I did so, and was answered by the senator the same as in the former interview, and with more emphasis. The streets were icy at the time, and Mr. Comstock had lost a leg, a good excuse for not venturing out. He appeared at the proper time and stood loyally by Spooner. Later I learned through Horace Reed, who succeeded me as court reporter and who had been Senator Spooner's private secretary and had done service as stenographer for Mr. Taylor during the campaign, that the letter from Comstock was received by Taylor as acting chairman of the committee. Evidently it was never given to Spooner, and he was not advised of its receipt.

While Spooner was in the Senate during the Harrison administration he secured for Mr. Taylor the appointment of commissioner of Pacific railroads. These roads had been advanced large sums besides being given extensive land grants to aid them in the construction. Bonds to the government were about to fall due, and Congress was appealed to to give up the first lien held by the government and take in lieu thereof a secondary lien and extend the time for a number of years. Henry A. Cooper of Racine was at the time a member of the committee to which the matter was referred, and I deem it fair to say that he studied the record of the relations of the companies to the government and familiarized himself with it thoroughly—and it was very voluminous—and joined with a minority of the committee in opposition to the proposed plan. Mr. Taylor favored it and tried to persuade me to vote for it. He said among other things, that unless we passed the bill the government would have to take over the roads. He was the only person who approached me on the subject. I was somewhat surprised when I read Mr. Cooper's statement a few weeks ago that Thomas Reed had threatened him if he opposed the measure. I had reason for being surprised, for I had a seat just behind Tom Reed at the time; was, I may say, intimately acquainted with him. He knew very well that I was opposed to the measure, but he certainly did not try to persuade me. Did he credit me with more stubbornness than Hal Cooper? But the latter deserves more credit than any other member for the defeat of the bill. We talked the matter over and I insisted that he must take the floor on the subject, which he at first seemed reluctant to do. I think it was his maiden speech in the House. He informed me the day before the matter was coming up that he was not prepared, to which I replied that if he would tell the House what he had told me he would defeat the bill. He took the floor, exhausted his hour, his time was extended, and the bill was defeated by a respectable negative vote. The result was that the government received its due, which, if memory serves me correctly, was over two hundred million dollars in principal, besides interest. It was undoubtedly Cooper's greatest service to the country during the thirty years and more that he has been a member. Taylor's prophecy failed.

I took my seat in the Fiftieth Congress just after the Holiday recess in January, 1888, having been prevented by illness from appearing in December. The House had organized, but no further business of importance had been transacted. John G. Carlisle of Kentucky was the speaker, the House being strongly Democratic. It was the Congress of the Mills bill. President Grover Cleveland had in his message denounced the Republican protective tariff and recommended radical changes. There was no question as to the attitude of President Cleveland on matters he discussed. William F. Vilas was a member of his cabinet. Spooner was in the Senate; also "Uncle" Philetus Sawyer. Among my colleagues from Wisconsin, the veteran in service was Lucien B. Caswell; another was Richard Guenther, elected from the Second District while a resident of the Sixth—the only case of the kind in the history of the state. Robert M. La Follette represented the Third, having first been elected in 1884, defeating E. W. Keyes and George C. Hazelton, a former member, for the nomination, and Judge Burr W. Jones, Democrat, after service of one term, in the election. Other members from Wisconsin were Henry Smith, Socialist, from Milwaukee; Thomas R. Hudd, Green Bay; Charles B. Clark, Neenah; Ormsby B. Thomas, Prairie du Chien; and Isaac Stephenson, Marinette. The Wisconsin members were all agreeable, and good fellowship prevailed. Among my first acquaintances was William E. Mason of Illinois, a clever and humorous individual. We lived with our families at the same boarding-house, and sat at the same table.

KNUTE NELSON

I had some slight acquaintance with Mr. Nelson before meeting him in Washington. He was first elected to Congress from Minnesota while I was railroad commissioner. There was a bitter fight over the nomination and election in his district. As he had before moving to Minnesota served one term in the assembly in Wisconsin, the opposition evidently thought capital might be made against him by examining his record. An agent sent to Madison for that purpose called on me one day at the state capitol and told me frankly his errand. I said that I had always heard Mr. Nelson spoken of in the most flattering terms, and that I thought his errand was in vain. He examined the legislative record of the year but evidently found nothing to his purpose, for nothing further was heard of it. Mr. Nelson was courteous and obliging, and went with me to look for living quarters.

His district took in practically all of northern Minnesota, including Duluth and the north shore of Lake Superior. Superior was just at the beginning of a boom, and considerable jealousy existed between the two cities. Duluth had the larger population and by far the greater business at the time. The Superior harbor had not been developed except at the Duluth end. A canal constructed through Minnesota Point near the Minnesota shore served as the entrance for vessels coming to Superior as well as to Duluth. Duluth interests conceived a plan of building a bridge between Minnesota Point from outside of the canal to Rice's Point, which would obstruct or materially hinder vessels from reaching the harbor then in progress of development at West Superior. There was no conceivable purpose in a bridge across the bay at that point other than to embarrass Superior. Mr. Nelson introduced the bill without any knowledge on my part. He was an old member serving his third term, while I was just beginning my first. Either I accidentally discovered its existence after it had been favorably reported by the committee, or it was called to my attention by Superior parties, and it was up to me to defeat it. It was considered a "private" or purely local bill, and such bills were generally called up just before adjournment for the day and unanimous consent asked for consideration and passage. Mr. Nelson had the ear of Speaker Carlisle; his general standing with the members of the House was good and popular. He was a good fighter. But the bill had to be defeated, and I was the only one directly interested.

This was in the summer of 1888. The discussion of the Mills bill was on and lasted for some weeks. I was not surprised when one afternoon just before adjournment Nelson called up the bill and the title was read by the clerk. I promptly objected to unanimous consent, and the bill went down. I suggested to Nelson that if he could secure a little time so that I might have ten minutes to explain the local situation I would agree to its consideration. But this he refused to do, and it may have been doubtful whether the time could be obtained. Of course the committee reporting the bill had only the Duluth side before it. One day La Follette and I together with our families attended a baseball game. As the afternoon sped on I excused myself saying that I had better get back to the House before adjournment to watch Nelson and his bill. Bob thought there was no danger. But I went back and sat in the lobby out of sight. Sure enough, Nelson, not seeing me on the floor, called up the bill, which again went down under my objection. The Republican national convention was coming on in Chicago, and many members left Washington to attend it, among them Nelson. I was urged by La Follette and others to join them; but, as Cleveland said of Congress, I had Nelson "on my hands," and could not abandon the post. An evening had been set aside for the consideration of private bills to which there was no expected objection. Such a session came on during the absence of Nelson and many other members. I attended with watchful ear, when to my surprise the Duluth bill was called up by Charles F. Crisp of Georgia—an entirely unexpected quarter. When I objected Mr. Crisp promptly withdrew his request and came over to me, stating that he had been assured there would be no objection, and apologized. That was the last of that bill, and the result met with universal approval in Superior at least. My own view then and now is that the bridge would have hindered that free navigation within the bay of Superior which best served both cities at the head of the lakes. It was short-sighted, to say the least, for the best interests of navigation there.

I had occasion to aid both cities with another bridge bill during the last term of my service. The ore industry of the Mesaba Range in Minnesota had been developed and a railroad was being constructed to carry the ore to the docks on Allouez Bay, the eastern end of Superior Bay. The House was then Democratic, and C. F. Crisp (the same Crisp) was the speaker. I had served on the fighting committee on elections with Crisp before he became speaker. The Duluth district was represented by a Democratic member. He had introduced the bill and we were in agreement on the subject of the necessity of the bridge. The consent of Congress was needed to authorize its construction across St. Louis Bay, a navigable water. My Democratic friend was unable to obtain recognition; the date of final adjournment was drawing near, when matters are pressing, and it was therefore difficult to get recognition for any but the most urgent measures. The Great Northern, or a subsidiary, was building the road and was about to construct expensive docks, all of which would be delayed if the bridge was not authorized. Crisp had been the leading member on the committee on elections during the Reed speakership, when the fight was bitter, and while we had been on opposite sides politically, our personal relations had remained very friendly and I had during his speakership received at his hands more than my share of recognitions. My Duluth friend, Mr. Baldwin, who seemed to have lost favor with his Democratic speaker, came to me in his distress and said that as he was unable to get recognition I must try it. When I approached Mr. Crisp he stated, as I had expected, that he had given me many recognitions, all that I could reasonably expect; all of which I acknowledged. But I represented the urgency of the measure not only to the localities but to the ore-shipping interests of the Great Lakes generally, adding that the bill had the approval of the War Department in all its details, etc. He stated that it would be useless, that even the time necessary to read the bill would invite objection. I said I should have to take my chances as to that. In order to remove the last objection I laid my case before Joe Bailey of Texas, a popular leader on the Democratic side, believing that he felt friendly to me personally. He had expressed his regrets when he learned that I was not coming back after the expiration of the Fifty-third Congress. He said, "But what can I do?" I suggested that when the clerk began reading the bill he direct some inquiries to me as to its merits—whether it had the approval of the War Department, etc.—and if the answers were satisfactory, that he ask unanimous consent that the reading of the bill be dispensed with. That plan was successful and the bridge bill was passed. This later bill was undoubtedly of far more benefit to both cities at the head of the lake than any other bill sponsored by the Duluth interests, and I have taken it out of its chronological order because it throws light on the local situation and because it helped to remove the unreasonable rivalry between the two cities which gave rise to the Nelson bill of 1888.

Nelson was an industrious and indefatigable worker in the interest of his district. We remained friends after the preliminary controversy referred to. On the whole he had the respect and good will of his colleagues, even though in the 1888 session he departed to some extent from the Republican fold and voted for the Mills tariff bill after making a speech in its defense, in which he advocated what he called a tariff for revenue with incidental protection. This was considered by the Republican protectionists a somewhat inconsistent attitude, their view being that to the extent that the duties protect American labor they do not provide revenue, and that in order to provide revenue they must admit foreign imports, which means giving foreign labor employment in preference to the American workingman. In other words, to the extent that it protects it does not produce revenue, and to the extent that it produces revenue it does not protect. Such was the theory of "Pig Iron" Kelley of Pennsylvania, and also of his Democratic colleague Samuel J. Randall, leading advocates of the protective theory in that and former Congresses. It was probably the only important legislative question upon which these two veteran legislators agreed. Randall had been speaker in a former house and was chairman of the committee on appropriations, which ranked in importance next to that on ways and means, the latter being the agency for raising revenue and the former for spending it.

Nelson retired voluntarily from Congress in 1888, later returning to the Senate, where he served with distinction until his death a few years ago. He had been governor of his state in the meantime. Before his election to that office we met accidentally in Minneapolis one day and had lunch together. He had not then announced his candidacy. I made the remark: "You can be nominated for governor if I read the press of Minnesota correctly, if you give your friends a little encouragement; but it is somewhat like you to sit back and expect the nomination to be handed to you on a platter." He laughed and replied: "Haugen, that matter is being attended to."

The Mills bill was the outstanding measure before the Fiftieth Congress. It was supposed to be an ideal Democratic tariff bill, but it did not fail to remember home people and left the tariff on sugar undisturbed, although the country imported during 1888 almost seventy million dollars' worth of sugar, apparently offering a good example of the principle of a revenue tariff, in harmony with the English system of levying duties on those articles not adequately produced in the home country. But the Louisiana sugar planter was too vociferous to be ignored. And my friend O'Ferrall from Virginia, although advocating strongly the revenue principle, made an exception of sumac growing on the mountain slopes of his state and used in the tanneries. Speaker Carlisle left the chair to support from the floor the passage of the bill. Robert M. La Follette answered him, devoting his time to that one purpose, and received the compliments of his Republican colleagues.

Being a new member I did not obtrude myself much on the time and attention of the House. I had read before entering politics Horace Greeley on protection and free trade, and had become convinced of the benefits of the protective principle for this country at least, and of the necessity of a developing country to make itself independent economically as well as politically. So it was easy for me to agree with the generally prevailing Republican attitude. The fact that I disagreed with Mr. Nelson on the question no doubt had something to do with Mr. McKinley (the leading Republican member of the committee on ways and means, and the floor leader in the debate) securing for me time to present my views. I had the usually allotted hour. Mr. Kelley listened to me, and when I closed came to me and paid me the compliment that I was one of the few younger men who fully grasped the underlying principles of the protective theory. Sam Randall, Democrat and former leader of his party, made a strong speech on the question in opposition to his party. His hour expired before he had finished, and he asked for more time. His Democratic friends refused him the courtesy; when McKinley, the Republican leader, who was to close the debate for the minority, said: "I give the gentleman as much of my time as he may want." This gallant offer was followed by tremendous applause in the galleries and by the Republicans on the floor. McKinley was always the courteous and obliging gentleman, popular with his colleagues. Mills was a ready and vigorous debater, but more of the fire-eating style. In closing the debate on the bill bearing his name, he marched down the aisle and with arms outstretched dramatically exclaimed: "Now, let the portcullis fall!" He had evidently read *Marmion*.

Some public lands in the then territory of Oklahoma were being opened for settlement and the bill on the subject, presented by William Springer of Illinois, who was chairman of the committee on public lands, excluded from the privilege men of foreign birth who had not resided in the United States at least two years. I moved to strike out the words "have resided in the United States for two years and." In presenting under the ten-minute rule my reason for the amendment, I said in part: "Whatever may be said as to the foreign-born citizens of our large cities, no complaint has ever been heard in regard to those settled in country homes." When I had finished, Mr. Springer adopted my amendment and the lands in Oklahoma were placed on the same basis as public lands elsewhere.

I served on the committee on labor in this and following Congresses; also on some minor committees.

TOM REED

The outstanding figure in the House during my service was unquestionably Thomas B. Reed of Maine. He was the recognized leader on the Republican side, ever ready and ever clear in his views. I believe it fair to say that Reed was the biggest man in Congress for at least fifty years back, and that he ranked in mentality with the leaders of any day in our history; he was ready in debate and in repartee. As an illustration of the latter quality: McMillin of Tennessee was of the southern flowery style, and when one day he closed his address with the somewhat stale expression, "I would rather be right than be President," Reed chimed in: "You will never be either." He was a giant mentally, and physically as well; there was never any doubt as to his views or his power and lucidity in presenting them. I pride myself on the fact that I enjoyed his friendship much more intimately than fell to the lot of most members. This was due in part to the circumstance that in my later service I occupied a seat very near his.

In the session of 1888 a bill was introduced to refund to states—which naturally meant northern states—money advanced to the federal government during the Civil War. This was opposed by the former rebel states. To the credit of northern Democrats, they as a rule supported the measure. But the opposition was obstinate and obdurate. The bill was favorably reported, and there was a fairly good majority for it on the floor. There were enough opponents to order the yeas and nays, and a course of filibustering ensued which lasted for weeks and contributed much to the adoption of the "Reed Rules" of the following Congress. Under the Carlisle rules and ruling, one motion to adjourn could not immediately follow another—a rule generally observed. New business must intervene. But a motion to take a recess, or a motion that when the House does adjourn it be to a time certain, was considered new business. It took forty minutes to call the roll. The House was thus held up for weeks with purely dilatory motions, one following the other without end. The case becoming hopeless, an agreement was finally reached to pass the matter over until after the election, when Congress would meet in short session. It is strange that the old-fashioned calling of the roll by the clerk still prevails in the House. Tom Reed visited Paris one summer, and I heard him tell of the electrical method of voting in the French House of Deputies, which he thought should be installed in the House. We have it in our state assembly. But the privilege of filibustering is too precious to be abandoned even by a self-styled progressive. It keeps the individual in the limelight. That and endless talk by strong lungs have defeated far more desirable legislation than they have promoted. The measure referred to finally became a law, and Wisconsin collected several hundred thousand dollars under it during La Follette's service as governor.

McKinley must be mentioned as one of the outstanding members during my service, probably ranking next to Reed. But many others might be named: Cannon of Illinois; also old Tom Henderson of that state; Dave Henderson of Iowa, one-legged veteran of the Civil War, with rich Scotch brogue when excited; Governor Gear, also of Iowa; Dingley of Maine; Long and Lodge of Massachusetts; Funston of Kansas, who went by the designation of "Farmer" Funston. He was the father of General Funston. Houk came from the Republican Knoxville district of Tennessee; he had been an officer in the northern army during the war. Democrats with whom I became more intimately associated, from service on committees and otherwise, were Crisp of Georgia; Allen, the wit of the House, and Catchings of Mississippi; Blanchard of Louisiana; Kilgore, Bailey, and Mills of Texas; O'Ferrall of Virginia. In those days many of the members lived at private boarding-houses, and closer acquaintances were formed in that way. Both O'Ferrall and "Silver Dick" Bland of Missouri were at "our" house. Mr. Bland was the outstanding advocate of the free coinage of silver at sixteen to one, and had been for years.

Judge Holman of Indiana was the veteran in service in the House. When asked if it were true that no man had ever served thirty years in that body he said: "I believe it is, but I am going to try to do it." I think, however, he died before enjoying the distinction. Since his day, Joe Cannon has broken the record with over forty years of service, and our friend Hal Cooper has exceeded the thirty years, and seems good for several more. Holman was the "Great Objector," the watchdog of the Treasury. He was especially interested in any new project in the River and Harbor bill—ready with a motion to strike it out. In that bill on one occasion was a moderate appropriation for a harbor on the Ohio River, in Holman's district. No objection having been raised, Tom Reed arose and stated that he had expected an objection from the watchdog of the Treasury; "But the watchdog of the Treasury seems to be like other watchdogs; he does not bark at home folks." The House was always generous with its applause at sallies of that kind, without reference to party origin. Mr. Holman had seen long service, and his judgment of men and measures was respected. The morning after the nomination of Harrison for the presidency I happened to be in the same car seat with Mr. Holman on the way to the capitol, and asked his opinion of the nominee. He said that he knew Harrison intimately, that they had never agreed politically, and added that he was beyond question as able an attorney as there was at the Indiana bar—a great compliment from a leading political opponent. I believe it can be fairly said that there was more of the chivalric recognition of merit in political opponents in those days than at present, when personal bitterness is more in evidence.

Election was coming on, and I was renominated without opposition and without leaving Washington. Doctor Johnson was again my opponent at the election. But the state went Republican by the old-time majority. The House was Republican by the narrow majority of three when it convened in December, 1889. The "Solid South" remained solid as formerly, with one exception: a Republican was elected from a New Orleans district of Louisiana. I am not counting the border states as part of the "Solid" group. When asked how it had happened that he was not counted out by the election boards, the Louisiana Republican explained that he knew their methods, so he and his friends had placed armed men at the polls to see that a fair return was made, and that resulted in his receiving the certificate of election; that otherwise he would have been defeated in the count. He was a native of his state, which perhaps aided him—not being a "carpetbagger."

On our way to Washington some of the Wisconsin delegation headed by Mr. Caswell, including Mr. La Follette, Mr. Thomas, and myself, stopped off at Indianapolis and interviewed President-elect Harrison. We were met with cordiality at his house. Mr. Caswell acting as spokesman asked that Governor Rusk receive his friendly consideration for the post of secretary of war in his cabinet. Mr. Harrison knew Rusk from earlier service in Congress and had evidently kept track of his subsequent public career. He referred to the strike episode in Milwaukee and expressed the fear that organized labor would most vociferously object to having him in that position. "Jerry" Rusk was made the first secretary of agriculture, that cabinet office having just been created, and established a service commendable to himself and to the administration. Under the supervision of a capable man at the head of the veterinary department he published a book on *Diseases of the Horse,* which received the highest praise of "Farmer" Martin of Texas, who said on the floor that the three public writings which he valued most were the Bible, the Constitution of the United States, and Rusk's horse book. On an excursion to Philadelphia to witness the launching of the battleship *Oregon* I was in the car with the press representatives, and the suggestion was made that "Farmer" Martin be asked to address them on the "New South." When the old gentleman appeared and the subject was suggested to him, he replied in about these words: "Gentlemen, you may talk about the New South, but there ain't no New South. The South is as she always was."

THE REED CONGRESS

The Wisconsin delegation supported Thomas B. Reed for the speakership. Other candidates were McKinley of Ohio, Cannon of Illinois, Burrows of Michigan, each having a respectable following and all popular and well qualified. Mr. Reed was nominated on an early ballot, and his nomination was made unanimous in the usual way of conventions. No bitterness ensued, and in the stormy session following he had no firmer advocates of his policy than McKinley and Cannon. La Follette was placed on the leading committee of ways and means, with McKinley as chairman, the latter thereby becoming floor leader. I was placed on the fighting committee on elections, the leading committee in fact under the rule of precedence, as it involves the very membership of the House. Reed's views on the subject of filibustering were well known; he had repeatedly stated that a few members had no moral right to obstruct the orderly activity of the majority, and he had the necessary nerve to carry his views into practical effect. Changes were made in the rules so that a member present and not voting would be counted to make a quorum.

CONTESTED ELECTIONS

It was a common Democratic charge against this Republican Congress that there was an indiscriminate unseating of Democratic members to assure a Republican working majority. Having been a member of the committee and familiar with the record as presented to it, I have always felt that we acted with the utmost conservatism, and no Democratic member was unseated unless the evidence of election fraud was overwhelming. There were more than twenty contests. The House seated, if my memory serves me correctly, five Republicans and one Independent. One Democrat, Breckinridge of Arkansas, was unseated, leaving a vacancy. His opponent was not a Republican, but an independent candidate who had served notice of contest and was traveling about the district getting evidence to support his case, when on a certain evening he was shot through a window of the house in which he was stopping, and instantly killed. No motive of a personal nature was apparent for the murder; politics was the only solution. Mr. Breckinridge went back to the district and was reëlected; whether there was any opposition I do not remember. There was nothing directly connecting him with the murder except that he was the beneficiary; certainly good reason for the committee's action.

General Chalmers, of Confederate war fame, had been accused by the Union forces of having shot down their men when cornered near Vicksburg and trying to surrender. He had joined the Republicans and had become a candidate for Congress in a Mississippi district containing, I think, nine counties. He made a thorough investigation in five of the counties, and while the results in them seemed to show a sub-

stantial majority for him, it was not sufficient to overcome
the majority reported against him in the district. His
former Confederate associates did not hesitate to attack him
in the most vicious manner, using against him the old Union
charge of his brutality during the war. We reported against
him because he did not carry his investigation far enough to
show a majority for him in the district. I think it was in connection with this case that the following happened: At a
certain precinct it was charged that the negroes were intimidated from attending the polls. It appeared that bullets
came flying into the road in front of the polling place. The
Democratic explanation of this was an admission that it was
true, but that some young men were shooting at a mark, and
the range was such that the bullets happened to strike near
the polls—just accidentally! It was different in a case in
South Carolina, where the Democrats charged that the negroes had been intimidated. The polling was done at an
open window—which seems to have been rather common.
There was a separate box for each candidate. As many of
the negroes were unable to read, a smart colored man conceived the idea of placing the tickets between the fingers of
the voter in the order of the boxes. A darkey was sitting on
the limb of a tree where he could watch the proceedings. It
soon appeared that the officers were changing the position
of the boxes, when the sentinel would cry out: "Change dem
tickets!" But the officials drove him out of the tree, claiming
that he was "intimidating the negroes."

John M. Langston was a mulatto, or rather a quadroon,
of Petersburg, Virginia. He was a graduate of Oberlin College and the head of a colored normal school at Petersburg.
He contested for a seat in Congress, and I was entrusted
with the conduct of his case and wrote the report of the committee. The facts as established beyond question were as follows: The colored population was in a large majority in

most of the precincts of Petersburg as well as in other precincts of the district. In order to be absolutely fair (?) the voters were arranged in two columns, one white, the other colored, and they voted alternately—one white man, one colored, etc. But the officials challenged each voter, white or colored, as he presented himself, thus exhausting the time so that when the whites had all voted the time for closing the polls had arrived and a large number of negroes were left with their ballots in their hands. A couple of attorneys had taken it upon themselves to make a record of the proceedings. They marched the voters with their ballots across the street to a notary, and each ballot was deposited attached to an affidavit that this was the ballot which the voter had tried to cast but had been prevented from casting. There were enough of these ballots to change the majority from Venable to Langston. I so reported. Mr. O'Ferrall of Virginia had charge of the Democratic side. After some filibustering I called up the case one morning. Mr. O'Ferrall made the point of "no quorum." A call of the House showed just a quorum, counting O'Ferrall. All the other Democrats had fled from the chamber. The chair announced a quorum present and proceeded to put the motion to adopt the resolution, when O'Ferrall requested a division of the House and immediately shot out into the lobby, expecting thus to break the quorum. The speaker proceeded to count, when I addressed the chair asking unanimous consent that the request for a division be withdrawn. When I arose, McKinley, sitting a little in front of me, turned and said: "Don't interrupt him. He is counting." But it was no time to hesitate. Reed saw the point and, as there was no objection, declared the resolution adopted and Langston was immediately sworn in. Another colored case, that of Miller vs. Elliott from South Carolina, had been reported favorably, and Mr. Rowell of Illinois, having it in charge, called it up and Miller was seated before O'Ferrall realized his defeat. This provoked a colored man in the gallery to yell out: "Dat man Haugen he treed one coon and brought down two." A Democratic paper of Richmond stated it differently the next morning: "We have come to a pretty pass when the country is run by a Norwegian and a nigger." And I am not sure but it placed the "nigger" first. I think this was the last effort of the session to break a quorum by wholesale desertion of the chamber.

As to election frauds, Virginia was in line with the blackest South. The law provided that voters must register at the county seat in order to be entitled to vote, and the list of voters was posted in each district. In the case of Waddill vs. Wise it appeared that the lists were duly posted, but almost immediately a person following tore them down. When the voter appeared he found that his name was not on the list, and having had no notice he was debarred from voting—all under the cover of law.

Why do the southern states remain generation after generation in the Democratic column? Look, in contrast, at the states of the North. They change with the times and issues presented. There is not one of them, unless it be Vermont, that has not at times departed from the Republican standard. From my experience on the committee on elections I am satisfied that the same would be true in the South if the elections were as honest and free there as in the North. But the aristocratic spirit prevails, and the negro, no matter how intelligent, must be constantly reminded of his slave ancestry. Quite generally, if not universally, the county was the local unit and the county machine appointed the local election officials, thus keeping the party in control.

During my service Congressmen had no clerks, as at present, except during my last term and then only during the session. This resulted in laborious correspondence carried on by the members largely at their desks during sessions. Until the general pension law, based on age, was enacted in 1890, petitions for special pension legislation were innumerable. When Harrison was elected in 1888 the correspondence was still further increased by applications for appointments to local post offices, etc. I adopted the plan, and adhered to it, of letting the incumbent serve out a four-year term. John M. Allen of Mississippi, the wit of the House, said that he asked a Republican friend how he got along with the patronage question, and his friend mournfullly replied: "Oh, you see

> Johnnie runs the Sabbath-school,
> Levi runs the bar,
> Baby runs the White House,
> And—— it, here we are."

To explain, John Wanamaker was the postmaster general, Levi P. Morton was vice-president, and the owner of the leading hotel in Washington at the time, the Shoreham; and there was a baby in the President's family—a grandchild, I think.

While Harrison was an able chief magistrate, on whose record there was no blemish, he seemed to lack that personal attractiveness necessary to popularity. A little incident will to some extent explain. On a Saturday afternoon I fell in with Mr. Anderson of Kansas, who suggested that we go to the White House to hear the Navy Band play. We did so, and arriving found the President alone on the back porch. He remarked that he was pleased we had come, that the Saturday before he had been there entirely alone listening to the music. He was pleasant, but seemed to lack that geniality so characteristic of McKinley, or the robustness and readiness of Roosevelt. Muscle and brawn always appealed to Roosevelt. He was a member of the Civil Service Commission when I first went to Washington. I was about his height and weighed about two hundred. He always wanted to feel of

my muscle. I sent him on an errand once, to look up a
charge of violation of the civil service law. He attended to
it promptly and made report, satisfactorily explaining the
situation. He and McKinley were of opposite types, but
both were popular nevertheless.

The name of a post office in Trempealeau County had
been changed during the former Cleveland administration
from Strum to Tilden, for what reason I never learned. The
railroad station remained Strum, and the patrons of the office
wrote me asking that I have its name changed back to Strum.
I called at the post office department, and a lady clerk and I
made the change. When I called at the department on my
return to Washington after a summer recess, the clerk said
that Mr. Wanamaker wished to see me. I called at his office.
He had a record of newspaper clippings, out of which he dug
up an item published in an up-state paper in New York, ac-
cusing him of insulting the memory of Samuel J. Tilden,
Democratic candidate for the presidency in 1876. I explained the circumstances to him, and my belief that the Tilden name had in all probability never occurred to my constituents, and certainly had not to me. He was satisfied. I
mention this only to show how an entirely trivial matter may
annoy a great man.

The town of Erin, St. Croix County, had been from
earliest times a Democratic stronghold. It was related that
a soldier of the Civil War tried to vote the Republican ticket
in Erin but was prevented with some violence. He consulted
Judge Wetherby, at one time circuit judge and a shrewd old
Democrat, as to whether a man was not free to vote as he
pleased; and was answered, certainly he was. He went on to
state what had happened to him in Erin. The judge
scratched his head and said: "I shall have to look that up."
The story was told on the judge as I got it. But Erin remained Democratic, and at the special election in 1887 I did

not get a single vote in the town. During the Harrison administration, however, when I became the dispenser of post offices, I received a letter from a resident of the town requesting his appointment as postmaster in some office. I answered that when the present occupant of the office of Erin Prairie had served his four years I should be glad to remember him for that position, that postmasters were appointed only from the patrons of the office. He wrote an indignant letter, restating his stanch Republicanism—how he had labored for the party and especially for me at the winter election in 1887, and was entitled to some better office than the local one. I answered courteously, thanking him for his support, but had to regret that in his enthusiasm in my behalf in 1887 he had forgotten to vote himself, as the record showed no vote cast for me at that election. I lost a correspondent, and a supporter—possibly.

James G. Blaine was the secretary of state under Harrison. Hans Borchsenius, then a resident of St. Croix County, a good friend of mine, a Dane by birth, and a veteran of the Civil War, wished to be appointed consul to Christiania, Norway—not a very important position. I presented the matter to Mr. Blaine and before I left he said: "I think I can do that for you, Mr. Haugen." I went home for the summer, but failed to hear further in regard to Mr. Borchsenius. Returning to Washington in November I called at the department. The very first thing Mr. Blaine said on my entrance was: "I have not been able to take care of your friend Mr. Borchsenius." Rather remarkable that he should retain what must have been to him an unfamiliar name. But that was characteristic of Blaine. I mentioned this to a member from Ohio, and he told of a like event in his own county. Many years in the past Blaine had made an address at their county fair and had become much interested in a colt on exhibition. Some ten years later he was again at the fair, and meeting the owner of the colt called him by name and inquired how the animal had developed. He never forgot names or events. Mr. Borchsenius was later appointed one of the auditors of the Treasury Department. He died in Madison about twenty years ago.

I think it was in this Fifty-first Congress that Henry C. Payne, member of the Republican state central committee and a representative of the Chicago, Milwaukee and St. Paul Railway, approached me with regard to some railway legislation. I disagreed with him. He asked me how "Bob" stood on the question. I told him that Bob felt about it just as I did. He became quite peevish and remarked that the railroad he represented had enough influence in the district to defeat Bob. This was in 1890 and the campaign was on. He did not make any direct threat as to me. But I resented his talk and left him, going directly to the capitol and informing La Follette. Within half an hour Mr. Payne called me out and asked me not to tell Bob what had occurred, that he had spoken hastily. I replied that he was too late, that I had already told Bob. La Follette relates this in his autobiography, but says that I told him some months later. He sent me the manuscript of this part of his life story and I called his attention immediately by letter to the real facts, which he admitted, but said my correction had come too late, as the book was already in print. Bob was defeated in the election, but it can hardly be attributed to the railroad influence, as all my other Republican colleagues were defeated that fall, I being the only Republican elected from Wisconsin. The McKinley bill must be given the credit—or blame. It was passed very late in the session, and was bitterly attacked with all kinds of criticisms and misrepresentations— as to its excessive rates and resulting costs of imported goods, etc. A River Falls merchant said to me that they would

have to raise the price of sugar and coffee because of the Mc-
Kinley law. Asked why, he replied that a traveling man
had told him that the wholesale price would have to be raised.
I informed him that not only did we *not raise* the duty on
sugar, but we actually placed sugar on the free list whereas
formerly under the Mills law of 1888 the rate had been two
cents a pound, and coffee was left on the free list as formerly.

I know that the opinion prevailed largely in Wisconsin
that the Bennett school law was the main cause of the Republican defeat that year. But the party was defeated in
Minnesota, in Iowa, in Illinois, in Michigan, and in other
normally Republican states, where there was no Bennett law
issue. Governor Hoard was blamed for signing the Bennett
bill. It may have been an error politically, but its intent to
secure an English education to all the children of the state
cannot be condemned. The editor of a German paper in
Milwaukee came to Washington during the summer and
sought the opinions of the Wisconsin delegation as to the law.
I refused to be interviewed in condemnation of it. Some of
my colleagues did criticize it and Hoard, thus probably aid-
ing in his defeat as well as their own. The report went
through the opposition press that a parochial school had been
closed in Jackson County because of the Bennett law. I had
a meeting at Black River Falls and asked for information.
A man in the audience told me, before the meeting opened,
that he was one of the trustees of the Lutheran Church and
was also a member of the school board, and that when the
time for opening the common school arrived it was mutually
agreed that the parochial school should close; that this was
done and that the Bennett law had had no influence upon
their action. I naturally spread this information as fast and
as far as I could. There was no doubt much more feeling on
the subject of the Bennett law among the Germans than

among the Scandinavians. The incident referred to in Jackson County occurred in a Norwegian community.[1]

I did not leave Washington to attend any of the conventions which nominated me, if Congress was in session at the time. My personal part in the campaigns was conducted by correspondence. I never had any personal controversy with a political opponent during campaigns, but was always able to meet him, shake hands, and have a friendly talk. I may make one exception. In 1890 Mr. Bailey of Eau Claire was my opponent. On several occasions during the campaign I saw him on the railroad platform and tried to approach him, but he avoided me. I had known him well during my days as court reporter and our relations had been friendly. He had, however, made some threats of impeachment proceedings against Judge Barron because of the latter's personal habits, which in fact had had something to do with my resigning as reporter of his court, as I did not wish to be involved in an investigation of a man who had befriended me and with whom I had maintained the closest personal relations. The charge never came to a head, and Barron served as judge I think until he died.

At the convention which nominated me for Congress the fourth time a resolution was introduced condemning the free use of railroad passes by members of Congress and other public officials. My good friend A. R. Hall of Dunn County, who had been chairman of the congressional committee in my preceding campaign in 1890, immediately arose and stated that the resolution was uncalled for as far as Mr. Haugen was concerned, as he knew that I had not accepted

[1] This statement may be belated, but the facts related by me, while written from memory, can be substantiated by reference to correspondence preserved from the time of my entry into politics. I have not gone over it in detail, but shall leave it in the care and custody of the State Historical Society. There will be a slight break caused by loss in the Capitol fire in 1904. The failure to make more thorough investigation of my correspondence in preparing these memoirs is due in part to the accident of breaking my right arm while engaged in the work. If health and life permit I may take up the correspondence more in detail later.

passes since my first entry into Congress. The resolution was withdrawn. Mr. Hall had been the leader in the movement in opposition to free passes in the legislature, never having accepted one himself. He may truthfully be said to have been the father of the "Progressive" movement in Wisconsin. He had before coming to this state been a member of the legislature in Minnesota. He was a manufacturer on a moderate scale in Wisconsin, had seen the evils of corporation favoritism in rate making, and was well equipped to lead the new movement. I enjoyed his intimate friendship and, I believe, his unlimited confidence. When he was chairman of the congressional committee I sent him a small sum to defray necessary expenses; this he promptly returned to me. I may say the same thing of Mr. Linderman of Trempealeau County, who had occupied the same position in an earlier campaign. Both rendered their services as a duty of citizenship, without looking for reward even to meet expenses.

But to return to Congress, which we left in charge of "Czar Reed." The Reed Rules were in force, so members in their seats refusing to vote were counted as present to constitute a quorum. A Democratic member from Ohio, who had formerly served as lieutenant governor of his state, joined with his Democratic friends in opposing this practice. But to his dismay Reed was able to refer to his record as presiding officer of the Ohio senate, where he had himself adopted the same plan. The so-called morning hour was largely consumed for weeks by some member of the minority taking the floor and exhausting his time in abuse of Tom Reed, the Czar. Reed never winced at this; it fell like water off a duck's back. When time expired, his gavel fell with the announcement: "The gentleman's time has expired." Mr. Springer of Illinois, who had been quite active and vociferous in this performance, was called away at one time, probably to look after his "fences." A member from Missouri thereupon took his place to flay Reed during the morning hour. One day Reed noticed that Springer had returned. He called a member to the chair, rushed down and greeted Springer, stating how glad he was to see him back. Springer did not know what to make of it, but Reed explained that he had had the gentleman from Missouri on his hands and felt like welcoming Springer to the old post.

Time wore on with discussion of the McKinley bill, necessary appropriation bills, election contests, and routine legislation, so adjournment did not come until well into October. The campaign was thus unusually brief. Compared with later tariff measures enacted by Republican administrations, the McKinley law was moderate in its rates, but like the Mills bill of the preceding Congress it defeated its proponents. Evidently it is easier to attack than it is to defend a measure of this kind. And that may be true generally in political contests; an aggressive critic can drag in any matter, however remote and irrelevant, while the defense is limited to acts performed. McKinley himself was defeated; La Follette, a member of the committee, likewise. When we met for the short session in 1890 I took occasion to express to Mr. McKinley my regret at his defeat. His reply was that he had no regrets, that it would probably be for the best. He may have had in view then what actually occurred—he was elected governor of Ohio in the next election, which had much to do with his later promotion to the presidency. McKinley did not have the aggressiveness of Reed. Had he been the speaker of the Fifty-first Congress, there might not have been the bitter contests on the floor; but the narrow margin of the Republicans might have left the party impotent. McKinley would have been conciliatory, if possible. But the Reed Rules had come to stay, so they were in effect retained by the next Democratic House. In order to make it appear that they were not followed, the distinction was made that instead of the speaker counting a quorum, that official appointed tellers to count those present and not voting; the difference between tweedle-dum and tweedle-dee.

I continued to serve on the committee on elections appointed by Mr. Crisp, the new speaker, with whom I had formerly served on that committee. There were not as many contests as in the former House; southern Republicans felt it would be useless, and the party in that section fell into what a member of Cleveland's cabinet would have termed "innocuous desuetude." I may say that in this Congress, I think it was, I served on a committee having under consideration an airship. A man from Chicago had taken out a patent for an airship constructed of thin steel plates, his theory being that if the air were entirely exhausted so as to result in a perfect vacuum it would rise into the air. The ship was to be some four hundred feet in length, other dimensions to correspond. But he needed money and wanted an appropriation, which was refused him. However, he was granted space in the Navy Yard at Washington for his experiments. I never heard of him afterwards; he was an impecunious and, no doubt, unpractical inventor. I am reminded of an old friend in River Falls, also an inventor. Tom Hill had conceived the idea that he could invent an air pump to be applied to a bicycle which would compress sufficient air into the hollow tubes going down hill so that when released it would run the bicycle up the next hill, or aid in so doing.

William Jennings Bryan, the "boy orator of the Platte," came to this Congress. He was a member of the committee on ways and means. Bryan possessed all the elements of popularity, a fine physique, friendly attitude toward colleagues, and a remarkably pleasant voice. I always attended his meetings when he came to Madison in later years. During his last visit here I spent a half-hour with him in his room at the Park Hotel. Jerry Simpson ("Sockless Simpson")

of Kansas, another member, was very much misunderstood.
He was elected as a Populist. A man of much more than
ordinary capacity, even for a Congressman (whatever that
may mean), he was ready in debate and full of statistical information, a seeming characteristic of his party. Both Bryan
and Simpson became popular with the members on both sides.
When the latter was taken severely sick, general solicitude
and sympathy were expressed on all sides.

Bourke Cockran of New York came into this House.
When the adoption of the rules was considered he defended
the Reed position because it gave the majority the right to
act. He said, "If you give me the power to obstruct the will
of the majority I may take advantage of it," or words to that
effect; but he denounced obstruction for the purpose of defeating the popular will as legally expressed. He was a
vigorous debater, and personally and naturally a good friend
of Reed's. Both observed that decorum in debate which
might be expected from men so eminent in their profession.

Reed undoubtedly had the presidential bee. But Blaine
from his own state still suffered from the same malady and
resigned the position of secretary of state under Harrison
because he saw some slight hope of attaining his life ambition
in 1892. But Harrison was renominated, and Blaine died in
1893. Before I left Congress in 1895 Reed asked me as to
the probable stand of Wisconsin Republicans in 1896. La
Follette seemed to me to be closer to McKinley than to him,
and I so stated. He remarked that McKinley's elevation to
the presidency "will continue the old régime at the other end
of the capitol," referring to the Senate, which he thought
was arrogating to itself more power and influence than was
warranted by the Constitution, and was encroaching on the
powers of the President. Have matters improved?

There were many applications for establishment of post
offices in my district, and it was often left to me to suggest

to the department names for them. I selected those that seemed to be in harmony with the population of the neighborhood, calling one in Burnett County, Freya; one in Pierce, Viking. But when I suggested Finland for a Finnish community in Douglas County some of the native Americans objected, deeming the name too chilly, and it was called Poplar at their suggestion. George Smith had moved from Eau Galle, Dunn County, and started a country store in Barron County some ten miles north of Rice Lake on the Omaha Railroad. An application came to me for a post office at Smith's store. I took it to the department and, as no preference had been indicated by the petitioners, I suggested Smithville or Smithfield. But there were too many Smiths already represented by post offices. I stated the objection to my correspondents, and was informed in due time that they had agreed on the name Haugen. I was able to tell Mr. Phipps of the Omaha Railroad a few years later that while I was not boasting about the size of my town, it was much larger than Phipps, named after him.

In my last campaign for Congress in 1892 a newspaper at Iron River in Bayfield County charged me with having supported a bill extending the exemption of Northern Pacific lands in Wisconsin from taxation. At a meeting in Iron River I challenged the statement and referred to the fact that the act in question had been passed before my first term in Congress began. Spooner was a candidate for governor at this election, and as he had been in the Senate at the time referred to I immediately called his attention to the charge, which was leveled against him as well as against me. I received no acknowledgment from him; but it undoubtedly cost him some votes in the northern part of the state. The editor retracted his charge as to me. Many years later Lincoln Steffens, who was then more or less engaged in the "muckraking" business, called on me in Madison looking for Spooner's record on corporation matters of this character. I told him that all the information I had was that the bill referred to had been passed before my service and I thought without a record vote. Spooner was defeated by Peck, who had defeated Hoard two years earlier. But Spooner came back several years later, was elected to the Senate, and served with distinction for a number of years. He was known to have been the attorney of the Omaha and other railroads in court and before the legislature. A long service in that relation would no doubt influence the views of most men and make them see matters from their client's viewpoint. It is human nature. This would be especially true in a man so intensely bound up in his client's case as was Spooner during his professional career. Quaere, whether a man so constituted would act impartially, though honestly, where the public and the corporate interests conflict.

Senator Sawyer was of the old-fashioned lumberman type, congenial and pleasant in his personal relations, but not free from those prejudices that seem naturally to accompany the possession of wealth. My relations with him were always friendly, and when the breach occurred between him and La Follette I was unable to determine whether the old gentleman was really guilty of trying to reach the court corruptly through La Follette, whose brother-in-law was the sitting judge in the state treasury cases, or whether La Follette jumped at a hasty conclusion and later adhered to it, seeing political advantage in so doing. It may be stated that the state treasurers had been in the habit of pocketing the interest collected from deposits of public funds in banks. Mr. Sawyer was one of the bondsmen, and the responsible one. Action had been brought by the attorney general under the Peck Democratic administration to collect the interest thus appropriated. There was no charge that the bondsmen had benefited by the action of the treasurers. Naturally

Sawyer tried to avoid the liability. Tom Reed asked me what there was to the row between La Follette and "Uncle Philete." I was somewhat noncommittal, and said that I had no reason to doubt Bob's word but I felt reluctant to believe that the Senator would try to reach the court in that crude way. Reed scratched his bald head and remarked: "You can never tell about these old commercial fellows." The occurrence was some time after Bob left Congress, when he was in the private practice of law at Madison. Sawyer lacked entirely that dignity generally ascribed to the members of the United States Senate. Tom Mills, who had been a member of the Wisconsin Assembly and later studied law in New York, came to Washington accompanied by two well-dressed New York women, mother and daughter. They called on me and I invited them to lunch at the Senate restaurant. As we passed Senator Sawyer's committee room I suggested that we step in and call on him. We had a pleasant visit, and as we were leaving Uncle Sawyer remarked: "Now, ladies, if you don't care about lugging your duds about with you, just leave them here in my room." Still the true lumberman! I always found him accommodating and ready to go to the departments if he could be of assistance. Naturally I did not court any misunderstanding with him.

Superior was the one place in my district that called for special attention and legislation. It was developing as a commercial city. The harbor was a long, shallow bay. The Soo locks were being deepened from fourteen to more than twenty feet, and Superior and Duluth harbors were crying for recognition in the same direction. Baldwin and I had asked the proper committee to provide for the necessary preliminary survey, but in vain. In considering harbor improvements the order was to move up the Great Lakes, Wisconsin thus preceding Minnesota. When Lake Superior was reached I proposed an amendment for a preliminary survey and estimate to deepen the Superior harbor to (I think) twenty feet. Mr. Catchings of Mississippi had the bill in charge and, addressing the chair, said he agreed to the amendment, which was adopted. Mr. Baldwin immediately came over to my seat and asked for a copy of my amendment, and when Minnesota was reached proposed a similar one for Duluth harbor. But Mr. Catchings now objected; why I never learned. But I intervened stating that the amendment now proposed was identical with one to which he had agreed a few moments earlier; and Mr. Catchings consented. Thus the preliminary step for deepening the two harbors was provided for. I have a surmise that Mr. Catchings had a very friendly feeling toward me personally, as I had at an earlier session when a member of the committee joined in a report in his favor when his seat was contested. He was an able lawyer and had served as attorney general of his state.

The free coinage of silver had been a prominent subject before Congress for many years. As a compromise the so-called Sherman law for the purchase of four and one-half million ounces of silver bullion monthly had been enacted. But this large market for silver had resulted only in its fall in value as compared with gold, and in the summer of 1893, instead of being sixteen to one it stood at twenty-two or more to one. Cleveland had been elected in 1892, and in the summer of 1893 he called Congress in special session to meet August 8, one of his avowed purposes being to repeal the so-called "purchasing clause" of the Sherman law. A long controversy arose over the entire coinage question. The Republicans as a rule stood with the President, while his own party was largely arrayed against him, many of the southern Democrats joining with the silver-producing western and mountain states. The Populists declared for free coinage. Some of the Democrats who had in former sessions favored free coinage now changed tune and supported the President.

Among them was Colonel Patterson of Tennessee, who appealed to his Democratic colleagues to come to the support of the President, calling their attention to the fact that the Republicans were supporting him. This provoked "Private John Allen" of Mississippi to say that, as for him, he was not elected to follow Republican leadership, that on the contrary he was sent to fight the Republicans, and he continued in about these words: "The gentleman from Tennessee reminds me of a certain Confederate colonel of cavalry who encountered a troop of Yankees, and not being able to hold his own turned tail and fled with his command down the pike. The Yankees pursued, and now and then a Johnnie would turn in his saddle and fire back. The Colonel got excited and called out to his men: 'For God's sake, boys, stop your firing; don't you see it only makes them madder!'" The story had been told on Mr. Patterson before, but it brought down the House. A partial understanding was entered into by some of the Republicans that they would vote for free coinage at twenty-two to one. The voting went on by stages, but twenty-two to one was not reached; it did not satisfy the free silverites, and they submitted to defeat at an earlier stage. The question remained an issue and "The Crown of Thorns and Cross of Gold" speech of Bryan at the Democratic convention in 1896 made him the standard bearer and free coinage at sixteen to one a leading issue in the campaign. Senator Jones of Nevada published his own speeches on the subject in book form, making a very respectable volume, showing great research and study—probably the most thorough exposition of the free coinage view put before the public.

John Lind of Minnesota entered Congress at the same time I did, and we became good friends and generally agreed on public questions. Lind was a student of economic questions, a wide reader, and a well-informed man. He was in-

clined to vote for free silver, but agreed to delay his preference until twenty-two to one, which was about the market
ratio at the time, was reached. But as it was not reached, not
being satisfactory to the more radical silverites, he remained
with the majority of the Republicans. In 1896, however, he
supported Bryan on the silver issue. He wrote me before
the convention that unless the Republicans did something for
silver he would sever his relations with the party. He served
as governor of Minnesota, and one term in Congress as a
Democrat from the Minneapolis district. In 1890 he was
the only Republican elected from Minnesota, as I was from
Wisconsin. I see him occasionally, when we renew acquaintance and review old times.

Mr. Pickler, a member of the House from South Dakota,
was quite a ready if not a very profound debater, and always
seemed anxious to contribute his share to the *Record*. This
provoked Reed to say of him: "I never understood what the
Bible meant by the wild ass's colt until I met Pickler."
(This was an aside, however, not for the *Record*.) While
Reed was always ready, and at least as clear and instructive
in debate as any other man of his day, he had the faculty of
not taking himself too seriously, and delighted both sides of
the House with his ready bon-mots. Somewhat in line with
this was a story told me in regard to Mr. Pettigrew of South
Dakota. Mr. Pettigrew was a man of ability who served as
a Republican both in the House and later in the Senate with
credit to himself and to his constituents. But the silver bug
got him; he left the party, became very much dissatisfied with
the general trend of affairs, and became a chronic growler.
I took part in the campaign in South Dakota—I think it
was in 1898. A woman at Millbank told me that during a
misunderstanding between her little boy and one of his play-
mates she heard one of them say: "There you go, pettigrew-
ing again."

The Republican Fifty-first Congress created a number of new states, and I voted for the admission of the two Dakotas, Montana, Idaho, Washington, and Wyoming. While this was a Republican Congress, the vote was not strictly partisan. It might have been expected that these states would remain in the Republican column; but some of them were affected by the free-silver virus, and most of them voted for Bryan in 1896.

In 1892 I was urged by some Republicans in the district to let my name be used as a delegate to the national convention at Minneapolis. But I declined, writing them that I appreciated the suggestion but thought it only fair that the honor should be conferred upon some private individual and not upon a member of Congress. This was different from what we have seen recently, when the present Senators and their immediate henchmen called in by special invitation nominated themselves as delegates. And they have the effrontery to call that the will of the people! I have witnessed national conventions, but never participated in one as a delegate. The Republican party of Wisconsin of today may truly be said to have fallen into the hands of "the three tailors of Threadneedle Street" who solemnly declared, "We, the people of England," etc.

Many interesting matters came up in Congress during my term of service, and I was a fairly close attendant on the sessions. No matter what the question under consideration might be, there was usually some member familiar with it and ready to inform the House. As said by Tim Campbell of New York, "A man ought to stay in the House, for every three or four days something interesting is said." This was intended as a compliment to a body in which talk was the order of the day.

I broke the rule in the Tenth District by serving four terms, all my predecessors having dropped out after serving three. I enjoyed the associations made. It was a pleasant experience. But under the then prevailing caucus and convention system I felt that there were ambitious members of the party, men of ability and standing, who would with reason aspire to the position. Whether I might have been renominated is scarcely worthy of conjecture. I am not aware that there was any criticism of my official action by Republicans, and it was a propitious time to step out. It has been difficult to select what ought and what ought not to be included in these personal sketches, but I have found it as difficult to get out of Congress, metaphorically speaking, as it was to get in.

CHAPTER IV

THE YEARS 1895 TO 1901

While I was in Congress it was the custom to give the widow of a Congressman one year's salary—then five thousand dollars. William T. Price, my predecessor, had always opposed the practice, so when he died in office I was in doubt as to the course to pursue in the case of Mrs. Price. In the dilemma I consulted Mr. Randall, then at the head of the committee on appropriations, an old member, former speaker, and one of the leading Democrats of the country. Mr. Randall asked me to look up recent precedents for him, and added: "Whatever has been done for other widows we will do for Mrs. Price." The precedent seemed unbroken. I introduced the necessary bill; Mr. Randall looked after it in the committee, and Mrs. Price received the money.

I had been fairly successful during my congressional career in obtaining consideration of matters of special interest to the Superior part of the district, the only section where special legislation was needed. Friendly expressions from Superior assured me of continued support from that quarter. The district had been changed after the census of 1890; Eau Claire and the counties to the south and east had been taken off, and Chippewa and Sawyer had been added. The Eau Claire lumber interests had been exchanged for the Chippewa Falls lumber interests, the largest being the Weyerhauser, known as the Mississippi Lumber Company, operating not only on the Chippewa but throughout the northern part of the district. I had served one term in the new district, although John J. Jenkins had been presented to the convention in 1892 as the candidate from Chippewa County.

I had been mentioned occasionally for the governorship, but had given the matter little attention. Peck had defeated Spooner in 1892. The Treasury cases had contributed to the defeat of the Republican state ticket in 1890 and 1892. But the Democratic administration had laid itself open to severe criticism because of the "Roster Printing" scandal, and everything looked favorable for the Republicans in 1894.

I had kept up a friendly correspondence with La Follette after his retirement from Congress in 1891. A. R. Hall was a true and trustworthy friend. He continued as a member of the Assembly and must be considered the prime mover in the legislative reforms then urged and later placed upon the statutes. He had been active in stopping the issue of passes to public officials, including members of the legislature. He was entirely unselfish in his public service, and well deserved the recognition later given him by the legislature in placing a tablet to his memory in the assembly chamber of the capitol. I think I brought him to the attention of La Follette. In a letter of December 26, 1892, I said: "I wish our legislature would pass some law similar to the British corrupt practices act, to purify and control the use of money in elections. I know in my own case it is a constant struggle to avoid being bled to death during a campaign both before and after convention. I do not believe (*inter nos*) that I shall ever be a candidate again, but it is getting to a pass where there is danger that the nominations will go absolutely to the highest bidder. Consult with my good friend Mr. Hall of Dunn, and help him get up a bill with this in view. You will find him an excellent fellow, and I wish you would get well acquainted with him. He is as honest as the day is long, and an invaluable member, watch-

ful and fearless." Mr. Hall became and remained until his death in 1905 a strong supporter of La Follette.

My term in Congress terminated on March 4, 1895. During the winter of 1893-1894 I had quite a large correspondence with La Follette, in which he urged me to become a candidate for governor. He assured me of strong support from Dane County and his old congressional district. But Hod Taylor had taken up his residence in Madison, having become the owner and editor of the *Wisconsin State Journal,* and had announced his candidacy for the gubernatorial office. Senator Spooner too had moved from Hudson to Madison, and it was to be expected that their political alliance would be exerted against any ambition directly or indirectly nourished by La Follette. They had always worked in harmony with Senator Sawyer. I had maintained the friendliest relations with the latter while he continued in the Senate, and felt that I had enjoyed his good will although he knew of my friendly relations with La Follette. I had never expressed myself concerning the controversy between them, except as heretofore mentioned, in conversation with Tom Reed.

Governor Hoard had expressed himself in favor of my candidacy. But I wanted further assurance before committing myself; so I took a trip to Madison to confer with La Follette and Hoard. Together we went to Milwaukee and had a conference with Horace Rublee, editor of the *Sentinel.* That paper had always spoken well of my record as a public official. Mr. Rublee was friendly personally, but was closely allied with the dominant faction within the party, represented by Henry Payne of the state central committee, Senator Sawyer, Senator Spooner, Elisha Keyes, and others. On the way to Milwaukee I told La Follette and Hoard that I would not become a candidate if Sawyer was going to oppose me because of his personal quarrel with Bob, and

that I wanted to interview him personally as to his expected
attitude if I became a candidate. To this both of them
agreed, Hoard perhaps with more readiness than La Follette. On May 24 I went to Oshkosh, where I had a pleasant
visit with the old Senator. I returned directly to Washington and on the twenty-seventh wrote La Follette. Let me
quote from that letter as to my visit: "You know I went
to Oshkosh and had a visit with the old man. I want to say
for him that he does not refer to you with that bitterness
which I have noticed in his conversations heretofore. On the
contrary, when your name was mentioned he said, 'I would
not do anything to hurt La Follette. On the contrary I
would do anything I could to help him.' I want to say this
to you because I think you would admit that the old gentleman is kindly disposed, and any controversy between him
and you will, I am satisfied, not be kept alive by him. He
naturally feels well toward his fellows, and that characteristic found opportunity of expression in my visit with him
the other evening. He is enjoying himself at his home,
where he has a great many friends and where his old age is
made as mellow as possible. I judge by his conduct that he
is well pleased with my candidacy. He said that he did not
expect to take any active part, but that he would take pains
to be interviewed if my opponents tried to make it appear
that my candidacy is an assault upon him and his friends."

The above was written when the facts were fresh in my
mind, and the interview was a determining factor in my candidacy. That the Senator was honest in his expressions at
the time I have no reason to doubt. If he had expressed himself in the least degree hostile, or had advised me not to enter
the field, I should have taken advantage of the suggestion.
He was a power in his section of the state, not only by
reason of his political influence but because of his extensive
business relations.

But the Madison Junta was not idle, and through its influence Hans Warner was induced to become a candidate. He must have realized that he stood no chance of being nominated even if I were out of the way. The hand of Taylor was too apparent. The convention came on July 27. The Dane County delegation was secured for me, but only by a slim margin. Taylor carried the city of Madison, but the outside precincts won the day, to his great disappointment. But I lost Pierce County to Warner. Senator Sawyer appeared at the convention marshaling his forces against me. His friendly feeling expressed in our interview did not meet with the necessary reciprocal feeling on the part of La Follette, and it is plain that their quarrel became the determining element which resulted in my defeat. While La Follette gave me the strength to enter the field, his feud with the old gentleman was the certain cause of my defeat.

William H. Upham, a lumberman from Marshfield, became the nominee for governor; he was, in fact, chosen by Sawyer and his following. I have not examined the newspapers of the day, but my recollection is that I was next highest in the outcome and led Hod Taylor by a fair margin. He came into my room in the Pfister Hotel, very much excited, and with an oath said, "If it had not been for you, Nils Haugen, I would have been nominated for governor today." To this I answered, "If that is so, Hod Taylor, I have rendered the state of Wisconsin a great service today." Mr. Grevstad, editor of the *Skandinaven,* was sitting on the bed with me, and H. S. Comstock of Cumberland and other friends and supporters were present, all of whom enjoyed the retort. My next visitor was "Uncle" Sawyer. He shook hands and said, "I am very sorry, but I had to do it on account of La Follette." I believe the old man was in earnest, and that his activity was entirely due to his controversy with Bob. The natural instinct of the latter was to be vituperative in disagreement. This was made more manifest in his later life. Sawyer added that they wanted to place some Scandinavian on the state ticket, and asked me who it ought to be. He said he would leave that to my choice. I suggested Sewal Peterson of Barron County, and he was nominated for the state treasureship. Peterson had been a county official in Dunn County before moving to Barron. He had represented the latter county in the assembly and had proved to be an able and efficient public servant. Another little matter that contributed to my choice of him was this: In the summer of 1893 he and I were on a fishing trip in Ashland County. His name had been mentioned for state treasurer, and I told him that he probably would be nominated. He replied, "But you may be a candidate for governor." To which I answered that that was not very likely, and added: "If I am, you will have to keep out of the way." He said, "If you are, I am for you." And he kept his word, and his county voted for me throughout.

After this head-on collision with Hod Taylor I recollect meeting him only once, and that was somewhat accidentally on the streets of Seattle in the summer of 1909. We had a friendly visit; no reference to former political controversies. He had secured an appointment to visit and examine our consulates abroad and was returning from a trip on that errand to China and Japan—around the world. He belonged to the old style of politicians who had dominated the state for years, generally led and supported by the "timber barons" of the northern part of the state. He had elements of attractiveness and sociability. He was probably opposed to me from the time I failed to support his friend Keyes for the senatorship in the legislature of 1879. The appointments he held in later years were obtained through the influence of Senators Spooner and Sawyer.

La Follette seemed more disappointed than I in the result of our campaign. He took no part in the fall campaign on account of failure of health. I felt it my political duty to support the nominee of the party, and did so, putting in some time in different parts of the state, visiting New Richmond, Merrillan, Glenwood, Viroqua, Soldiers Grove, Deerfield, Racine, Marinette, and other places to which I was sent by the state central committee. My good friend Dave Henderson from the Dubuque district, Iowa, had asked me to come into his district for a few meetings; so I spent the last ten days of the campaign there, meetings being held at Delaware, Quasqueton, Cedar Falls, Popejoy, Iowa Falls, and some other places. Whether I was of any service to my friend is not for me to say, but he was reëlected by a good margin. Later he was speaker of the House. He was a one-legged veteran of the Civil War. Although his district was not among the strongest Republican districts in his state, he was one of the few Republicans saved in the wreckage of the party in 1890. He was a firm and steadfast friend and supporter of Tom Reed and Joe Cannon. He died in service in the House.

I attended the short session of 1894-1895, closing my congressional service on March 4 and bidding farewell to numerous friends. I know of no one now living who served with me from Wisconsin, except Hal Cooper, who served during my last term and is still a member. There may be others, but if so they have, like myself, fallen out of the public eye.

I went back to my home in River Falls and settled down to the practice of law, which I had not entirely abandoned during my public service; I had retained an office and had tried to keep up my law library in a moderate way. In a country town like River Falls the building up of a law practice is naturally a slow process, but the practice is fairly reliable when once established. The fees are necessarily more moderate than those charged in larger cities. During the six years devoted to private practice I built up a clientele that afforded me a fairly sufficient income for family support, and its growth was steadily increasing each year, in spite of interruptions. I could not keep free of political activities, and as each primary approached I was more or less drawn upon by requests to take part, which it was almost impossible to ignore in view of friendly interests in former campaigns of my own. River Falls is a prosperous community, and my associations there were pleasant. During the season I could indulge my sporting instincts by fishing in the Kinnickinnick, this much of the time with my good friend Fred Burhyte, a leading merchant of the city. The stream was then fairly well supplied with the native speckled trout. Now the speckled is a rarity, the German brown and the rainbow having driven out the smaller trout. They are perhaps as gamy; but I cannot help feeling that the speckled should have been protected in many of our streams which seem its natural breeding places, and where it had always propagated and thrived. I think I was the first one to plant young trout fry from any state hatchery in Pierce or St. Croix waters, which I did personally on a very cold March day (in 1883, I think) while I was railroad commissioner, placing some in Rush River, some in the Trimbelle, and some in the south fork of the Kinnickinnick. The Izaak Walton League of River Falls has been very active of late years in keeping at least some of these streams well supplied and thus attractive to anglers. Not being overrun with clients, I could generally leave the office about five o'clock in summer and have a plentiful catch for breakfast the next morning. I find that in writing to La Follette at a later date I used this language: "I attend strictly to business—and waiting for it."

The campaigns, both state and national, of 1896 were

coming on. The leading candidates for the presidency seemed to be William McKinley and Tom Reed, both well-known friends of La Follette and myself. On the question I inclined to Reed. I quote from a letter to La Follette of December 18, 1894, which fairly presents my views of the two candidates at that time. Reed had made some friendly allusion to Sawyer, which irritated Bob. I wrote: "Reed said in a letter to me about what you attribute to him. I hope, Bob, that you will not let that influence your action. I do not think it ought to. Sawyer went down to Chicago to induce Reed to come to Wisconsin, and the letter was written with that visit fresh in Reed's mind. I know that he has the friendliest feelings for you. I think that he is likely to be the nominee, and that it would be very bad policy for us to antagonize him. I do not know that he would be the nominee if the convention were coming off today. I doubt it, but he will be the leading figure of the next House as its speaker, and his course will be wise and meet general approval, especially in view of the fact that the Democrats have endorsed his former methods, and the large Republican membership will be for him, and I look for public sentiment to move strongly in his direction. . . . So I think you ought not to let anything that Reed may have said with reference to Sawyer weigh with you in the least. You know I like McKinley personally even better than Reed, for the latter is sometimes as arbitrary and disagreeable as any man can well be; but I believe he is far greater than McKinley and that he is more likely to be the party nominee."

Such was my impression of the two men, and it has remained so ever since. Reed as president would have been entirely independent of any dominating influence "from the other end of the capitol," as he expressed himself to me in speaking of McKinley. Bob, however, when the time came threw his influence to McKinley. Mark Hanna became the power behind the throne, and as far as Wisconsin was concerned it meant Henry Payne and the Sawyer influence; just what Bob did not want. I had tried the task of peacemaker between La Follette and Sawyer, and had failed. Bob was relentless. He may have given his own interview with the old gentleman a hasty construction not intended. But it was not in him to retreat in controversy from a position once taken.

In the spring of 1896 by invitation of Bob we met with friends in Chicago to confer as to the approaching campaign. Judge Emil Baensch of Manitowoc was invited, and I think H. P. Myrick, editor of the Milwaukee *Free Press,* was there, as well as other political friends. The proposition came from La Follette that he, Mr. Baensch, and I all become candidates for the nomination for governor, with the understanding that we coöperate and support the leader of the trio in the convention. I had said that I would not be a candidate. Once was enough for me. Nor did I believe that the plan was practical. Delegates cannot be shuffled about like pawns on a chessboard. Baensch seemed to agree to the plan. I was asked not to turn the matter down then and there; but a few days later I wired both that I must be considered out of it. Both La Follette and Baensch went into the convention and were defeated. Edward Scofield of Oconto received the support of Sawyer and friends and became the next governor. They dropped Upham, their choice in 1894, after one term of service.

We supported McKinley for the presidential nomination, although I should personally have preferred Reed, for the reasons stated. It seemed easier to carry the state for McKinley, and we were not entirely blind to the practical side of politics. I visited Chicago during the early part of the campaign and called at the Republican national headquarters. Payne was in attendance as the committee member from Wisconsin and chief lieutenant of Mark Hanna, the chairman. I was introduced to Mr. Hanna, whom I had not met before, but who politely (politically) said he remembered me. A trick of the trade! He asked me to go to the state of Washington and take part in the campaign. I spent some weeks on the coast, visiting the principal cities on the Sound, also Aberdeen on Gray's Harbor. The places were somewhat familiar to me in name at least through the river and harbor bills in Congress. I had a pleasant outing and was treated courteously. The political agitation on the coast and in the mountain states at the time rested on the question of the free coinage of silver. Bryan had captured them in the Democratic convention with his "Crown of gold pressed upon the brow of labor" speech, and that section of the country supported him in the election. My expenses—all I ever charged or received in any campaign—were paid by the national committee.

Governor Hoard had the ambition to become secretary of agriculture under the McKinley administration, and we favored him. It was generally agreed that La Follette's relations with the President-elect made him the natural spokesman for Hoard. But Bob's health was such that he refused to take over the commission, so I was urged to go to Canton to see McKinley. This I did about holiday time. I asked the editor of the *Skandinaven,* Mr. Grevstad, to accompany me. We called at the McKinley home, where we were graciously received. McKinley was always the gracious gentleman and of friendly nature. When I presented the matter to him he confessed great admiration for Hoard, but said—what we knew—that Senators Spooner and Sawyer were very much opposed to him; that they had asked him to appoint Mr. Payne postmaster general; that with the opposition existing in Wisconsin he could not honor the state with a cabinet position. He added that the only request

Mark Hanna had made of him was that he make Mr. Payne postmaster general. Some time before this visit I had called on Senator Davis, at his request, in St. Paul. He knew I had served with McKinley and was on friendly terms with the President. He frankly stated that he had the ambition to become secretary of state. His service as chairman of the Senate committee on foreign affairs had made him familiar with our foreign relations. He was a scholarly gentleman. I had known him from my reportorial days and had kept up the acquaintance while in Congress. He asked me to mention him to the President, and this I did when nothing could be done for Hoard. But the same objection was raised as in Wisconsin. One of the Minnesota Senators was very much opposed to Davis; so the state must be passed over. I so reported. Davis was an "annexionist." As chairman of the committee he had advocated the taking over of Hawaii. Later, as one of the commissioners to the Paris Peace Conference after the Spanish War, he favored and advocated the annexation of Porto Rico.

After the election in November I received a letter (or dispatch) from a friendly editor in the northern part of the state asking me if I would accept the appointment of governor of Alaska. I answered as follows: "I have not thought seriously of asking for any appointment at the hands of the incoming administration, and am not prepared to say that I would want to be frozen up in Alaska. The only inducement for giving such a proposition serious thought is the fact that it might afford an opportunity to make some money. It is not desirable as a place for a family. But if I am governor of Alaska, you shall have the best post there is, and have the freedom of all the glaciers on the coast." Many years later I asked my friend if the proposition had come from Senator Spooner, and he said it had. It was evidently thought desirable to get me as far away from Wisconsin as possible, and it may have been expected that I would leap at the bait.

After McKinley's inauguration I had occasion to visit Washington and called at the White House. The President being occupied I left my card. Calling again the next day, I was received in the most friendly manner, with the remark, "You were here yesterday. Why did I not see you?" I replied, "You were busy, and I did not want to interrupt." He said, "The door is always open to you, Mr. Haugen," and expressed himself as always glad to see me. I did not look for position, knowing the uncertainty and the brevity of political appointments at best. A close friend and associate during my congressional service was Binger Herman of Oregon, a very popular member of the House. He had been appointed commissioner of the General Land Office in the Interior Department. I called on him, and he offered me a roving commission to visit and inspect the land offices in the West, adding that there were great opportunities to make money out there. I have no reason to think that he meant in any other than an honest way; but he had some difficulty himself later, being accused of participating in some speculation inconsistent with his official duties. He was acquitted of any criminal charge. The Senator from his state was under arrest but died before the case came to trial. I stopped over night in the summer of 1909 at Roseburg, his home town, and spent a pleasant evening with Mr. Herman. He seemed downcast but expressed himself as very much pleased at my stopping over to see him. He too passed away some years ago.

At the May, 1898, session of the circuit court in Pierce County some friends approached me suggesting that I enter the race again for the congressional nomination. We had a meeting in the office of the county clerk, who participated and declared himself enthusiastically for me. He had al-

ways been a loyal friend and supporter in previous campaigns, and I believe he was honest in his professions at the
time they were made. He had held the office of county clerk
for many years. Hans Warner had attended the state convention as a delegate in 1896, but became ill on the way
home and died a few days later. The field seemed open as
far as my home county was concerned. I was assured by my
friends at the meeting referred to that Pierce County could
be relied on without any concern on my part. To my as-
tonishment I was informed shortly before the county convention that the county clerk was a candidate for either secretary of state or state treasurer. I made no campaign in
Pierce County, but went to the county convention with a
delegation from the city and town of River Falls. Professor
W. D. Parker, for many years president of the normal
school at River Falls and always highly respected by all his
fellow citizens, had at my request agreed to serve as a delegate. He had never been an active participant in our politics, but having retired from the school he agreed to take
that much part. The convention met. The choice of delegates went on until about half of them had been declared
elected and they were against me. They were elected singly,
but it was understood whom they favored. The election of
another delegate was announced, when a friend came to me
and said, "Haugen, they are counting you out. The last
vote gave a majority for you." I had no active lieutenant on
the floor, so I arose and stated what I had learned. I asked
that a recount be had and that Professor Parker be permitted to verify it. This suggestion could not very well be refused me. Mr. Parker reported a majority of more than
half a dozen votes for me, just about the reverse of what the
tellers had reported. What should be done with the delegates
already reported elected? The ballots had been scattered or
destroyed. I then and there withdrew my candidacy, but

added that, although not a delegate, I would be at the state convention. The hand of the "Hudson ring" in putting up a candidate from Pierce—an old trick—was too evident. I had made no particular effort and had spent no money in this wild-goose chase, which I certainly would not have entered except for the assurance made by some of the men who helped to stack the cards against me in the convention. James O. Davidson was nominated for state treasurer at the state convention, which thus disposed of the aspirant from Pierce. This was my last appearance at a popular election, and I wired my friends in other counties of the district that I was out of the race. In Burnett, however, they persisted in electing a Haugen delegation. I could always count on Burnett; it had always been for me and remained true. My intimate friend of later years and now, Mr. Myrland, for the last sixteen years secretary of the State Tax Commission, was then district attorney of Burnett and marshaled the forces.

The ease with which this fraud was perpetrated on the voters even in a county as free from corrupt practices as I believe Pierce to be, naturally impressed upon my friends, as well as myself, the belief that some method better calculated to carry out the popular will than the free and easy caucus system ought to be adopted. There was no legal supervision of the old caucus and convention. Any political crime could be perpetrated and the guilty go unpunished. I still believe in the convention, as it is necessarily a part of our representative system of government; but it needs to be placed under legal supervision so far as the choice of delegates and voting are concerned. The primary election, as we have it, destroys party harmony and responsibility, and has resulted in the present chaos in Wisconsin. It would seem entirely practical to convert the present primary election of candidates into an election of delegates to conventions

under the same official supervision as now exists. I claim
to be a fairly intelligent citizen, but I am at a loss when making a choice from among a dozen or more candidates for a
county office. I cannot know all the candidates. Delegates
from the precincts would be able to confer at a county convention and impart information. It was the abuse of the
caucus that gave impetus to La Follette's advocacy of the
direct primary election.

I took an active part in the campaign of 1898 and supported Scofield in spite of the fact that he had shipped his
cow on a free pass from Oconto to Madison. I had opposed
the use of passes, but did not believe that the cow episode
was a sufficient reason for turning the state government over
to the Democrats. Scofield was reëlected.

I continued my practice and a quiet life at River Falls.
I had built up a fair practice which, if attended to without
too much interruption by politics, would assure a reasonable
living for my family. But once in politics it is difficult to
abstain entirely. Judge Bundy's term was about to
expire in 1897, the election of his successor taking place in
the spring of 1896. He had in my opinion made an ex-
emplary judge. He was of a hasty temperament, but that
had not shown itself in his career on the bench. There had
always been some opposition to him in his own county of
Dunn, perhaps due to his Democratic propensities before he
became judge. The opposition was very likely the result
of early party feeling. He had at his last election stated
that if elected then he would not seek another term; but as
another election approached he changed his mind and announced his candidacy. I was asked to meet in St. Paul
some friends from Dunn, Buffalo, and Pepin counties, which
I did. There were some attorneys in the group. They
asked me to become a candidate for the judgeship—certainly
a very honorable position. But my personal relations with

Judge Bundy, as reporter and as friend, were such that I could not agree to be a candidate against him. I so told them. My friend Hall was of the group. Later E. W. Helms of Hudson became a candidate against him and was elected. I supported Bundy, as in his former campaigns. I preferred his personal esteem and friendship to the judgeship with his defeat, and have never regretted my course.

I had become allied with La Follette in 1894, and now that he had become an active and persistent gubernatorial candidate himself, he did not hesitate to draw on me—and on his other political friends. My consent to be a candidate in 1894 had doubtless aided him in his home county of Dane. He had made a valiant fight against Keyes, Taylor, and Spooner, and had won out with me as a candidate. The two of us had elements of strength which neither singly possessed. This he fully realized, as I certainly did. Though La Follette had become our standing candidate for the governorship, he failed again of the nomination in 1898; Governor Scofield was renominated and reëlected. Mr. La Follette was again a candidate in 1900. His persistent pursuit of the office, carried on uninterruptedly for six years, calls to mind the quatrain in *Hudibras* which reads:

> Honor is like a widow, won
> By brisk attempt and putting on,
> With entering manfully and urging,
> Not slow approaches like a virgin.

The "widow" yielded in 1900. He won the nomination and was elected by a large majority.

CHAPTER V

STATE TAX COMMISSIONER
RAILROAD ASSESSMENTS

La Follette was elected governor in 1900 by a plurality of over 103,000, the largest plurality ever received by him for that office. In 1904 he received a little over 50,000 plurality, or about half of that in 1900. He came to the office pledged to a reformation of the method of taxing railroads; also a reformation of our primary election system. The latter was more particularly of his own creation. Our old friend A. R. Hall had been a consistent and persistent advocate of the former for many years as a member of the Assembly. I know of no man holding more strictly to a straight course in public life than Mr. Hall. He was making some improvements on his place at Knapp near the Omaha track, and needed some gravel. The railway company offered to give him a load of it; but no, Hall would have no gift from that source. Naturally he was a strong supporter of La Follette.

I had settled down to my law practice, and did not look for any appointment at Bob's hands; the fact being that I saw nothing at his disposal inviting enough to take me from my private practice. Nothing had been said between us on the subject. A brief appointment would break up the business I had established, and necessitate starting anew at the end of the term. My friend Henry Comstock of Cumberland called one day, and evidently inquiring for the governor-elect asked me what I wanted in the line of appointment. I answered him that I could see nothing I could afford to accept under the circumstances. He asked: "How about assistant tax commissioner?" The position of second assistant was vacant, as I knew. I said that I could not afford to break up at River Falls and move to Madison for a three thousand dollar position. That had been the former salary. He called my attention to the fact that the salary of that position had been raised to four thousand dollars—an amendment I had not noticed. Think I said I might consider that. Just what authority Mr. Comstock had I do not know. I heard nothing further about the matter. On the day of the inauguration of the new state officers in January I was at Ellsworth trying a case. Mrs. Haugen, however, was in Madison, where our daughter was attending the University. She was present at the ceremonies at the Capitol and congratulated the new governor. He said: "Where is Nils?" She replied that I was at Ellsworth attending court. To which he said: "Oh, the rascal!" I received a message from him a day or two later requesting me to come to Madison. I complied, and he offered me the position of second assistant to the tax commissioner. The commissioner was Norman S. Gilson, a former circuit judge of the Fond du Lac circuit; and, by the way, he was a brother of my former law partner, F. L. Gilson, at River Falls. The latter was a Republican, while the judge was a Democrat, and was the representative of that party on the commission. The first assistant was George Curtis, Jr., of Merrill, an attorney of long practice and good standing. Former Congressman Michael Griffin, of Eau Claire, with whom I had served a term in Congress, had on his retirement from that body been appointed tax commissioner by Governor Scofield. Griffin died in 1900, and Judge Gilson was promoted to the head of the commission. An interim appointment of Colonel William J. Anderson, who had served as his private secretary, was made by Governor Scofield to the second assistant's place, but his appointment had not been submitted to the senate, thus leaving the matter open for La Follette to withdraw his name and substitute mine, which he did, I having agreed to accept the position. My service began the first of February, 1901.

THE TAX COMMISSION

As already stated, Mr. Hall had been hammering away at the matter of the taxation of railroads, and it had become a leading issue in the campaigns. Bills were introduced in the legislatures to increase the license fee, or to place the roads on the ad valorem basis—that is, to subject them to taxes upon the value of the property, in the same manner as the "general property" of the state on the local rolls. In the session of 1897 an apparent compromise was entered into. I have this from Mr. Hall. The suggestion was made in the committee that a temporary commission be appointed to study the whole problem of taxation and to report to the next session. The representatives of the railways agreed to this, and agreed further, that they would abide by the judgment of such commission as to their special interests. This seemed a happy solution all around, and the bill was passed. The governor appointed as commissioners Burr W. Jones of Madison, K. K. Kennan of Milwaukee, and George Curtis—certainly a commission that commanded respect. Mr. Jones we all know. Mr. Kennan had had much experience in tax matters—tax titles, sales, etc.—in northern Wisconsin, and the same can be said of Mr. Curtis. Their report to the governor and legislature in 1899 was thorough and comprehensive. Assessments generally were found to be inaccurate and without system or uniformity. Gross undervaluations were the rule on the part of the local assessors, the county boards, and the state board of assessments. The state board consisted of the secretary of state, state treasurer, and attorney general. The law had always provided that property should be assessed at its true and full value, and this applied to all assessing officials. While the state board had never, except I think in one instance, found the general property to exceed $630,000,000 in value, this commission found that its value was at least twice that. They also found that there was just reason to believe that railroads were not paying their due share of taxes.

The most important feature of their report, however, was the conclusion arrived at, that the question was of such magnitude that a permanent commission ought to be created for general supervision of all tax matters, to study the question and to make further recommendations. The result was the creation of a commission consisting of three members to serve for a term of ten years. Why the life of the commission was arbitrarily fixed at ten year it is difficult to conceive. The commission thus created was the one of which I became a member in 1901, and on which I continued to serve until May 1, 1921. Although my name appears in the report of the commission of 1901, that report was prepared and ready for the printer before I entered upon my duties. My predecessor, Colonel Anderson, must have credit for its recommendations, and not I. That report confirmed the views of the former interim commission.

My colleagues on the commission were pleasant and agreeable men to work with. While there necessarily arose differences of opinion as to values and methods of procedure, the action was always friendly and without bitterness. Attorneys learn to yield to defeat; it is part of the experience of the profession. Judge Gilson was less of an investigator than a judge. His experience on the bench had accustomed him to hearing cases as presented, and he was more likely to overlook his duties as an investigator than was Mr. Curtis. The latter was alert and industrious. The Judge was also less inclined to assume duties imposed by law, by questioning the authority of the legislature to confer upon the commission powers which might be considered legislative or judical.

Judge Gilson was *the* commissioner, and as such was by act of 1899 made a member of the state board of assessment. In 1901 the duties of that board were transferred to the tax commissioner and his two assistants, the three having equal authority as members of such board. In all other matters the commissioner had the sole power.

In his message to the legislature in 1901 Governor La Follette recommended legislation impressing upon the tax commissioner the duty to "enforce the provisions of the law, that all property be placed on the assessment roll at the actual cash value," etc. But when the new state board, consisting of the three commissioners, in the state assessment of 1901 increased it from $630,000,000 to $1,436,284,000, he balked. Such valuation would more than double the mill tax levied for the common schools, and it struck him with fear for its political results. Thus does politics make cowards of the bravest reformers! The commission had recommended to the legislature that the mill tax be reduced to one-half a mill, as the results of full-value assessment were readily foreseen. It also suggested as an alternative that the school tax be placed at a fixed amount of $700,000. But neither of these suggestions was followed. Later the tax was reduced to seven-tenths of a mill, where it remains. To me the duty of the commission seemed plain. Judge Gilson yielded to the Governor and suggested that we reduce the state assessment to forty-four per cent of the value we had found to be the true one. Curtis seemed at first inclined to follow him. I stood out. The Governor sent for me and rather insisted on an arbitrary reduction. I asked him, as I had my colleagues, if the language of the law was open to construction. While it was admitted that it was not, the apology was that the former board had set the precedent, and it had better be followed. Just what we were expected to remedy! Time to make the state assessment was at hand, and Mr. Curtis asked me to let the matter go over, as he wished to be away for a few days. I readily consented. When he returned he called me up one evening and said that he had been thinking the matter over and had come to the conclusion that I was right and that we would have to follow our full-value assessment. This relieved me, but placed Gilson on the anxious seat. He evidently informed the Governor of the changed situation in the commission. I was again sent for and the old argument repeated. Perhaps Bob thought that, as I was his appointee, I ought to yield to his wishes. He did not say so; but a few mornings later Herb Chynoweth, a leading attorney of. Madison and a warm friend of us both, asked me to call at his office. I did so. He said: "Nils, you will have to yield to Bob on the matter of the state assessment. He insists on it." This provoked me and I answered in about these words: "You had better tell Bob to call for my resignation. I will be ――― if I will violate my oath of office for him or anybody else. Do you think this law is open to construction?" He, like the others, could not say that it was.

I heard nothing further from the Governor, and Curtis and I made the state assessment. Judge Gilson did not join in that assessment or in that of 1902. He filed a statement in the first year in accordance with his views. The record for the two years bears this out. This action of the board had an important bearing on the assessment of railroads at a later date. Had the state assessment not been held up to full value, the assessment of the railroads would have been upset, because the tax rate applying to them was based upon a full value of the general property of the state. So Curtis and I saved the railroad assessment plan advocated

by La Follette and recommended by the commission.[2] It
is fair to state that after the first two assessments Gilson
joined in the results.

Every investigation made confirmed the conclusion of the
earlier commission that the assessment laws were violated in
entire defiance of the full-value requirement. Iowa County
had been assessed the best of any county, at about ninety-
six per cent of what seemed to be full value. A revaluation
of the assessment units had been made by order of the county
board. One county in the northwestern part of the state indicated less than twenty per cent. Real estate and personal
property as well were rising in value and so continued until
about 1919. The rise was general and fairly uniform, counties maintaining their relative positions with surprising regu-
larity, which confirmed our belief in the reliability of the
data used. As a basis for real estate values, bona fide sales
were used and comparison made of the prices paid and assessments of the same property. While there can be no
absolute accuracy in valuations, this test is at least a fair
approach when applied to counties as units, and has been followed by a number of other states as the best thus far suggested. Wisconsin was a leader.

RAILROAD TAXATION

In 1901 the commission had placed before the legislature
two methods either of which would have increased the tax on
railroads: one was to increase the gross earnings tax; the
other to place railroads on the so-called ad valorem basis.
Each bill passed one house, but failed in the other. Judge
Gilson suggested that we renew the recommendations in

---

[2] See opinion of Supreme Court, *128 Wis. Reports,* where the decision by
Judge Marshall covers a large part of the volume. It bases the judgment of
the court and the validity of the tax largely upon the full value of other property
found by the commission.

1903. Fearing that the same methods might be pursued, I suggested that we had better take one horn or the other of the dilemma. This was done, and the ad valorem tax was recommended, and the law passed substantially as we have it now. As it was foreseen that the tax might be questioned and the state deprived of necessary revenue during litigation, the act provided that the companies if they disputed the tax should continue to pay the license fees as formerly, adjustment to be made at the final decision of the court. The license fee had since about the time of the Civil War been four per cent of the gross earnings of those roads whose gross earnings for the preceding year averaged $3,000 per mile. A lower rate was applied to those earning less than that average, those earning less gross than $1,500 per mile paying only five dollars per mile of road. Minnesota has adhered to the gross earnings tax, but has increased the rate to six per cent. It is no doubt a simpler method than finding the true value of large railroad properties extending into many states and apportioning it to each state. But the ad valorem tax seems more equitable in equalizing the tax burden.

By assessing the general property at its full value we had cut the average tax rate to less than half, and this was the rate levied on the railroad property. The full value also equalized the state tax of the different counties. Milwaukee County gained by the new assessments. I speak of that county as it approximated one-fifth of the valuation of the entire state. It had better assessments than the average county of the state; had more competent assessors.

We made our first railroad assessment in 1904. I had more to do with laying the foundation for our valuation than did either of the other members. To get a basis I went through the files of the *Financial and Commercial Chronicle* for a period of five years, noting down the number of shares of stocks sold each week and prices paid. The same method was pursued as to bonds. We had used a five years' average of sales in arriving at the value of real estate, and that period was used for railroads as well. By using such voluminous records erratic transactions could be ignored, as they were when discovered—the same as in real estate sales.

It was thought desirable to make some estimate of the *cost* of railroad properties in the state; and the commission secured the services of Professor W. D. Taylor of the engineering department of the University to supervise the work. The Chicago and Northwestern had no record of the cost of its early construction in Wisconsin, such records having been destroyed in the great Chicago fire in 1871. The companies readily agreed to make estimates of cost of reconstruction. The commission was limited as to expenses. The companies went over their entire lines, dividing them into sections. Mr. Taylor made an estimate of a sufficient number of the sections to make a fair comparison with their work. It was remarkable that a difference of only about two per cent separated them. The commission assessed the Northwestern at $71,500,000, and the Chicago, Milwaukee and St. Paul at $70,000,000. Cost of reconstruction indicated in each case about ten million less.

The result of this first assessment increased the revenues of the state by $545,912 above what the license fee would have been. The next year the increase was $666,879; and in 1906, $642,500. Hall's efforts along this line were fully justified by the results. Taking a few of the larger companies, the excess of tax over license fee in the first assessment runs as follows: Chicago and Northwestern, $200,-174.92; Chicago, Milwaukee and St. Paul, $235,473.39; Chicago, St. Paul, Minneapolis and Omaha, $57,653.27. A few of the smaller roads gained slightly by the new system.

Michigan had preceded Wisconsin in this method of assessing railroads. An action was brought by the railroads in the name of the Northwestern, contesting our assessment and resulting tax, which were sustained in toto by our supreme court. An appeal to the federal Supreme Court from the decision of the state court was in preparation. That action had been taken in Michigan, but before the railroads were able to perfect their appeal the United States Supreme Court sustained the action of the Michigan commission, which made the appeal here hopeless. As the interest rate on unpaid taxes was high, there was an immediate application made to pay. In fact the mail was too slow; the companies immediately wired to learn the exact amount, so that they could stop interest. We had no difficulty after that; railroad representatives appeared each year presenting their views, but the meetings were most friendly. While they argued for lower valuations, in general they approved our methods in that respect as well as in arriving at the tax rate.

TAXATION OF CREDITS AND MONEY

The poorest assessment of any class of property was unquestionably that of moneys and credits—intangibles. The law provided that the owner should submit to the assessor the average owned by him during the year; and while there was an offset of indebtedness against credits, there was no offset as to money. If a person owned on the average during the year ten dollars, or any other sum, it was taxable. Douglas County, having within it the city of Superior, did not for several years report a single dollar of money. Some other counties followed closely in its wake. This almost absolute failure to assess intangibles led my colleagues in the report of 1903 to recommend their entire exemption from taxation. A long argument with that end in view was prepared by Mr. Curtis and appears in the report of that year.

I dissented from the views of my colleagues and prepared a like lengthy argument presenting my views. But
Gilson was still the sole commissioner, and he refused to let
me publish it at length. Not to be outdone, I had it printed
in the Milwaukee *Free Press* and put in pamphlet form for
distribution, at a cost to myself of over seventy dollars. I
distributed the pamphlet to the members of the legislature
and to others about the state. I also appeared before the
Assembly committee on taxation. Mr. Dahl, later state
treasurer, was the chairman; Henry Johnson, also later state
treasurer, a member. The committee agreed with my views.
A brief statement was permitted me in the report, and the
following is a summary taken from it:

> Second. I do not agree to the broad proposition that credits are
> not property. There seems to be a difference of opinion among
> economists on the subject.
>
> Third. No state has yet exempted credits, and the step would
> be without precedent in this country.
>
> Fifth. It may be true, as the report states, that "direct taxa-
> tion of credits as property has long been abandoned in nearly
> every civilized country except the states of the American Union."
> The report does not specify the countries referred to. I have to
> some extent examined consular reports made to the State Depart-
> ment at Washington and published in 1888 on the subject of taxa-
> tion, and as far as my investigation goes I have failed to find a
> single country which does not in some manner impose a tax on the
> creditor, either in the form of an income tax or in some other way.
> They have substituted the creditor for the credit. Before exempt-
> ing credits it certainly seems reasonable that a thorough investiga-
> tion should be made in order to ascertain whether some method of
> reaching the creditor would not be as practicable here as elsewhere.
> This feature of the question the report entirely ignores.

I believe it absolutely safe to state that this was the very
first suggestion made of an income tax in any official or semi-
official document in this state. When the matter was discussed before the committee, Chairman Dahl said: "Will

you prepare an income tax bill?" He seemed ready to introduce it. I said that it might be premature, as a question of
constitutionality might be involved. "Well, will you draw
an amendment to the constitution removing the doubt?" The
result was that Dahl and I prepared such an amendment the
next day. This amendment was duly passed by the session
of 1903 and that of 1905; but due to an oversight in the office
of the secretary of state, it was not submitted to a vote of
the people until the election of 1908, when it received popular approval by a large majority. But this takes me ahead
of my story chronologically and the income tax must be
postponed for the present. It is true that La Follette recommended an income tax in his message to the legislature in
1903. My views were then before him, and he agreed with
me.

He had earlier, in 1901, recommended to the legislature
the separate assessment of the mortgagee's interest in land
to him, and such an act was passed. In his message in 1903
he said: "This may easily be done," etc. But as this was
in direct controvention of the terms of the contract, it was
plainly in violation of the constitution. So in a special message in 1903 he suggested the restoration of the mortgage
tax, "until such time as the legislature can pass a law for the
taxation of incomes to take the place not only of the taxation
of credits, but also of the taxation of most, if not all, other
personal property." But he suggested that the old law be so
amended as to "relieve the mortgage debtor of double taxation, pending the adoption of the constitutional amendment
for a graduated income tax." This was just what he had
been informed, and which as a lawyer he knew, could not be
done. He agreed with us when we conferred with him, but
persisted in repeating his former recommendations.

The work went on with reasonable smoothness in the commission, except that now and then Judge Gilson became

doubtful as to our authority. The legislature had passed an act authorizing the commission, upon complaint being made, to order a reassessment of any assessment district when, after a hearing, it was of the opinion that the assessment made was not in substantial compliance with the law and that the interest of the public would be promoted by a reassessment. The judge doubted its constitutionality and refused to follow it. When a complaint from the town of Iron River, Bayfield County, came before us, Curtis and I held a hearing and ordered a reassessment—Gilson not participating. The matter went to the supreme court and the act was upheld. This authority lodged in the commission helped very materially in securing better work on the part of local assessing officials throughout the state.

I was in constant confidential communication with the Governor's office in those days. Conferences of his friends were frequent. One matter that was supreme with him was the primary election law. On that he had set his heart. Some of us had doubts and expressed them. We thought that a safer course, and one more in harmony with our representative form of government, might be adopted, by placing the caucuses under legal supervision. But he countered with: "Give us this law and we can hold this state forever." He got his law, and held the state as far as he was concerned.

When it was suggested that he would run himself out of issues, Bob said, "Oh, we will always find issues."

THE RAILROAD COMMISSION

When we commenced to tax railroads under the ad valorem plan, the cry went up that the roads would recoup the additional tax by an increase of rates. In order to obviate this, La Follette recommended the creation of a railroad commission having full supervision of the reasonableness of

rates. This was done in 1905. The session was pretty well
along and no bill to that end had been introduced, when La
Follette requested me to draft a bill. It was no easy undertaking; but I went at it, referring to like acts in other states.
I copied from the law of Texas a provision by which no se-
curity could be issued by the company without the approval
of the commission—a "blue sky law." This provision was
struck out of the bill; but such a law was later enacted. I
was evidently ahead of the times. When it came to the appointment of a commission, I was again consulted. Bob had
in mind that he might find a man with experience in that
respect in some other state. First he thought of a member
of the Texas commission. But that idea was dropped.
Charles A. Prouty, from Vermont, was a member of the
Interstate Commerce Commission at the time, and his term
was about to expire. The impression had gone abroad that,
for some reason, Roosevelt would not reappoint him—probably because he was not in sympathy with Roosevelt's wing
of the party. But Bob, very anxious to secure him for Wisconsin, consulted with me and asked me to go to Washington
and interview Mr. Prouty. Late one evening I was called
up and asked to go at once. I replied that I did not have
money enough about me to take me to Washington. "Come
up to the Capitol, and we will get you the money, so you can
leave on the three o'clock train." I followed instructions and
went to Washington. Arriving there, I called on the Interstate Commerce Commission, of which Martin A. Knapp of
New York was then chairman. Judson C. Clements of
Georgia, with whom I had served in Congress, was a member. Mr. Prouty was at the time in Vermont on a vacation.
I was assured by both of these men, however, that the President would reappoint him, and that it would be useless for
me to see him with reference to a Wisconsin appointment.
But Mr Knapp said, and Mr. Clements approved: "You

have an excellent man in Wisconsin, well qualified for the
service. He has done some work for this commission, and
no better man can be found." They referred to Professor
Balthazar H. Meyer, then connected with our university.
I knew Meyer fairly well, and had the highest opinion of
him, but was glad to have this endorsement from such high
source. I was to some extent familiar with his work for that
commission, as I had had occasion to read his report of an
investigation made by him.

I returned to Madison and reported. Professor Meyer
was at the time in Europe, so Mr. La Follette cabled him
offering him the position, which was accepted. Halford
Erickson, now with the Byllesby Company in Chicago, who
had for several years been the chief statistical official of the
state, was selected as a member. Bob wanted me to become
the third member. I hesitated; really feared the senate
would think he was putting it on rather thick by removing
me from one commission to another. So I protested that I
had better remain where I was. Mrs. La Follette was
present. The fact was that the other commissioners had not
at that time been fully determined upon; at least I had not
been informed. Mrs. La Follette said: "You had better
tell Mr. Haugen who will compose the commission." I had
no objection to either of them. Bob assured me there would
be no objection to my appointment. I interviewed no member on the subject. My name was rejected by the senate.
No reason was given and none was sought by me. Four
Republicans had voted with the Democrats against my con-
firmation. I think the record bears me out in saying that
not one of them was returned to the senate at the end of his
term. I do not claim that my rejection had anything to do
with that; but it was at least a coincidence.

As stated in an earlier issue of this magazine, the tax
commission was appointed for ten years, with no provision

for its continuance after that time. By 1905, however, it became obvious that the commission must be a permanent body. The Governor so recommended, and the present law was enacted providing for three commissioners to hold office for eight years; the first three to hold for four, six, and eight years respectively. When it came to naming the commissioners Bob suggested that perhaps I had better take the short term, in view of my rejection for the other commission. But I insisted that I wanted the long term, and the senate might do as it pleased. The result was that I was given the long term, and no objection raised. At the expiration of my term in 1913 I was reappointed by Governor McGovern.

The members of the commission aimed to keep out of political activities. But we did not hesitate to discuss tax matters, which at that period were to some extent political. That fell directly within the scope of our duties, and we tried to keep the public informed. I also contributed to the party campaign in the state; and the demands for that purpose did not then shock the La Follette-ites. Their sensitiveness is of later birth; perhaps subject somewhat to political atmospheric changes, like old rheumatics. My last contribution to the La Follette campaign fund was in the spring election of delegates to the national convention in 1912. Of that later. It had a sequel.

CHAPTER VI

Taxation under the La Follette Régime

There was a certain timidity about Judge Gilson assuming administrative responsibilities. I have related how in the first state assessments he advocated a reduction in the valuation from that which the commission agreed was the true one, but when we came to fix the tax rate applicable to railroads, he went to the other extreme. He proposed to add to what had been determined in the state assessment to be the true and full value of the general property of the state an additional amount without assigning such amount to any county or to any specific class of property. To this I objected. Mr. Curtiss joined the judge. Having officially found the full and true value, I contended that the commission should stand by its action.

Under date of November 28, 1905 I sent the following communication to Governor La Follette: "In compliance with your request, of 22nd inst. for my views as to needed legislation on the subject of railroad taxation, I avail myself of the opportunity to submit the following:

"Chapter 237, laws of 1901, made the members of the tax commission the state board of assessment for the valuation of the general property of the state. It provided that the valuation of each county so determined 'shall be the full value' according to the best judgment of the board.

"When the assessment of 1901, being the first assessment made by the new board, was under consideration, some objection was urged against fixing the valuation of each county at what the board unanimously agreed was the full value of the property in such county. The majority of the board were of the opinion that the law was not open to construction and that the 'full value' meant the true cash value of the property, and not a percentage thereof. The assessments of 1901 and 1902 were made by a majority of the board, commissioner Gilson dissenting, considering the state board of assessment a board of equalization rather than one of assessment, although agreeing with the other members as to what was the true value in the different counties.

"Chapter 315, Laws of 1903, placed the assessment and taxation of railroads under the state board. No change was made in the law as to the duties of the board, making assessment of the general property of the state to place the valuation of each county at the 'full value' of the property therein; and in all state assessments subsequent to the one of 1902 the commission has been unanimous in placing such assessment at the 'full value' of each county.

"Chapter 315, Laws of 1903, relating to railroad taxation, provides that to ascertain the tax rate to be applied to railroads the aggregate of state and local taxes, excluding special assessments for local improvements, shall be divided 'by the aggregate true cash value of the general property of the state upon which said taxes were levied.' Sec. 14.

"For the purpose of ascertaining this 'aggregate true cash value of the general property of the state,' section 9 provides that the state board, now tax commission, 'shall, according to their best knowledge and judgment, ascertain and determine the true cash value of the general property of the state, assessed and to be taxed in the then present year' and section 10 provides that the board 'may *correct* the valuation of the general property of the state' for the purpose of fixing the tax rate for railroads.

"The commission has not hesitated in making the state assessment to consider property not upon the local tax rolls and which necessarily would not 'be taxed in the then present year' although the question in view of the language quoted is not free from doubt. The reason for the action of the commission in this respect is that any other course would reward counties omitting taxable property from the rolls at the expense of counties making more earnest efforts to have all taxable property placed upon their rolls. This increase in property not upon the local tax rolls has not been disturbed in valuing the general property under sections 9 and 10 referred to.

"Under the sections last referred to should the tax commission confine itself to a revaluation of the property upon the local rolls, and what is the limitation upon it under the language that it 'may *correct* the valuations'?

"Do these sections authorize the commission to add arbitrarily to the aggregate valuation of the state a lump sum without assigning such additional valuation to any particular county or to any particular class of property?

"The questions submitted may be more forcibly presented by referring to the railroad tax roll of the commission as to what actually occurred. The first railroad assessment was that of 1904. The valuation of the general property of the state last preceding such railroad assessment was $1,753,-172,000, and the total of taxes $20,640,543.16, making the average tax rate upon the citizen taxpayers of the state .01177325, or $11.77+ on each $1,000 of assessed valuation.

"The value of all railroad properties was fixed at $218,-024,900. At the rate given, the railroad tax of 1904 would have been $2,566,854. The board, however, resolved, 'that, in order to make the valuation or assessment of railroad companies made by the board just and relatively equal with the valuation of the general property of the state, the valuation of such general property be corrected by increasing the same $51,015,000, which amount added to $1,753,172,000 makes the total valuation of the general property of the state $1,804,187,000.' Page 53 Tax Roll.

"The increase thus made in the general property of the state changed the tax rate from .001177+ to .01144+, and being applied to the railroad assessment reduced the tax levied upon railroads from $2,566,854 to $2,494,232; a reduction of the railroad tax by $72,572.

"In the railroad assessment of 1905 the general property of the state was increased in the same manner. The reduction of taxes levied upon railroads in 1904 and 1905 amounts in the aggregate to $139,743.04.

"In justice to the railroads the commission should retain the authority to assess all taxable property in the state at its full value, and any doubt that may exist in the present law as to its authority to consider property not upon the local tax rolls should be removed. Justice to the general taxpayer requires that this authority be properly safeguarded. In reviewing the valuation of the general property of the state the tax commission should be required at least to state in what classes of property and in what counties the changes have been made. The railroad companies are represented by able, persistent counsel. Their principal efforts have been directed to securing increases in the valuation of the general property of the state. The private taxpayer is not represented. He must look to the commission for the protection of his interests. The acts of public officials should be open to public inspection and subject to just criticism. No intelligent criticism can be made of changes in valuations unless they are so subdivided and distributed as to indicate with some degree of particularity the nature and location of the property assessed."

I have recorded the foregoing at length, as I disagreed
with my colleagues. I have notes in detail of the action of
the commission in regard to the matter here related. The
records of the commission show that after 1906 the state assessment as made was used as the basis of the rate to be
applied to the railroads. My views prevailed in the end.

LA FOLLETTE AND DAVIDSON

James O. Davidson had been elected state treasurer in
1898, and reëlected in 1900 and 1902. He was a candidate
for renomination in 1904. But La Follette had a slate in mind
with Davidson as the candidate for lieutenant governor.
This did not appeal to Jim, and Bob was unable to persuade
him. The governor asked me to see Davidson, during the
state convention. Bob felt assured of his own renomination.
I made the appeal to Davidson that acceptance of the position of lieutenant governor would be pretty certain to land
him in the governor's chair; that Bob would in all probability
go to the United States Senate; also that Bob's health was
such that there might be a vacancy at almost any time, and
he himself would be governor. This persuaded him, and he
consented. Being a thrifty individual, he had naturally preferred to remain treasurer at $5,000 a year to holding the
lieutenant governorship at $1,200. But the allurement of
being governor won the day. He had been an original La-
Follette man and had so remained—a true and faithful supporter. The slate went through as Bob had planned. He
won, but not without considerable friction in the convention.
This was the so-called "Gymnasium Convention," when the
meeting almost broke up in a row. As will be remembered,
some of the delegates withdrew and later, under the designation of "National Republican," voted for ex-governor
Scofield at the November election. The latter received some

12,000 votes, and La Follette was reëlected, receiving some 50,000 majority over his democratic opponent. Davidson became lieutenant governor.

At Bob's request I drafted the platform for this convention. When asked to do so I said that I would not give unqualified approval to the Republican tariff law then recently adopted by Congress. He agreed. We deemed it extreme. From the beginning of my congressional service I always had had a keen interest in tariff legislation. During the campaign of 1888 there was published a volume entitled *Protection Echoes from the Capitol,* edited by Thomas H. McKee, assistant librarian of the United States Senate. It quoted freely from the debate on the Mills Bill to sustain the republican views on the subject of protection. I find myself quoted *fifteen* times; Richard Guenther *nine* times; Caswell, the dean of our delegation, *four* times, and La Follette *once.* None of the other Wisconsin members is quoted. While actively participating in political campaigns I devoted myself largely to discussion of the principles of protection, especially in the earlier campaigns. Later the free silver question received its share of attention. Since I served on the Committee of Banking and Currency, that came about in the natural order of things. Southern elections and suppressions of the Republican vote came to my attention as a member of the Committee on Elections, and was not omitted in the campaigns. These were questions that it had been a part of my duties to examine, but the protective tariff was with me an abiding interest. I put in the platform on the subject the following:

> *Tariff and trusts*: We firmly adhere to the fundamental Republican doctrine of protection to American labor, and believe that the aim of a truly protective policy should be to stimulate competition in the home market and not destroy it by favoring trust combinations. We therefore believe in a readjustment of tariff schedules in all cases where protection is employed for the benefit of capital and only to the injury of the consumer and workingman.

Mr. Hannan, private secretary to the Governor, went over the draft with me. He suggested some minor changes. The platform was submitted to the convention and, to our surprise, was adopted without dissent. This was the last convention for the nomination of state officers held under the old nominating system; and one of the noisiest.

As I had predicted, La Follette was elected United States Senator by the legislature in January, 1905. He remained, however, in the position of governor until the end of the year, taking his seat in the Senate January 4, 1906. So the forecast made to Davidson came true, although somewhat delayed. I suggested to Bob that he postpone his senatorial ambitions until the law became effective for the election of senators by direct vote of the people. But the legislature was favorable, and he took no chances, although an early and consistent advocate of the popular method. Davidson became governor at the beginning of 1906.

Irvine L. Lenroot had served as speaker of the Assembly, and had presided over the "Gymnasium Convention" in 1904. He had been a consistent friend and supporter of La Follette and was an able and alert legislator. When the next state election approached La Follette deserted Davidson, who naturally looked to a renomination as governor, and pressed the nomination of Lenroot. In view of the fact that I had been the intermediary in persuading Davidson to accept the lieutenant governorship in 1904, at Bob's insistence, I felt that it was at least unwise, yes, ungrateful, to deny him a reëlection, of which he was reasonably assured, if nominated. And there was nothing in his record which could possibly have changed the public opinion of him. A meeting of La Follette's friends was held in Madison, where I expressed myself to that effect, and was supported by my next door neighbor, Judge Zimmerman, a former partner of La Follette. I wrote Bob my views, stating that under

other circumstances Lenroot's candidacy would have my approval, that I recognized his ability and qualifications, but
that in view of our activity in persuading Davidson to accept
the minor office in 1904 we ought in good faith to stand by
him in 1906; also that pressing Lenroot inopportunely might
take him out of the public service, for which he was well
fitted; that as there was no apparent change in the public
view of Davidson, it seemed ungrateful to abandon him now,
and that he appeared to be sure of winning in the primary
and being elected in November. To this appeal Bob remained characteristically silent. I say this, as it seemed to
be a method with him not to answer letters that were somewhat embarrassing. My prediction came true. A year later
when we were walking down the street together one day,
Bob said: "Well, Nils, you are a pretty good fellow; you
haven't said, 'I told you so' yet."

Davidson was reëlected in 1908, and served until succeeded by Francis E. McGovern in January, 1911. Davidson did not possess that broad view of public affairs desirable in the chief magistrate of the state. His general education was limited, but he had good judgment, was naturally cautious, and sought advice. He had a splendid adviser
in his private secretary, Colonel O. G. Munson of Viroqua,
and left a creditable record as governor. He knew my close
relations with La Follette, and at first I thought he was a
little shy of me; but after a while I enjoyed his full confidence, and gave him my best advice when called upon. I
felt it due to the Governor to give him any support within
my power consistent with my official duties—a service to
the state rather than to the individual.

LA FOLLETTE'S ASPIRATIONS

My own course being so closely interwoven with the political life and ambitions of La Follette, I feel it necessary

to give him more space and attention than might otherwise
be warranted. No sooner had La Follette taken his seat in
the Senate than he discovered a star still higher in the political firmament, and the presidency became his consuming
aspiration. I first became aware of this in the autumn of
1907. The presidential election of the following year was
attracting public attention. While the press naturally gave
much space to the subject, very little, however, was devoted
to La Follette, except an occasional notice in the state newspapers. There was certainly no apparent popular demand.
I was therefore surprised when on a Saturday afternoon I
called at his farm home at Maple Bluff and found a number
of his friends consulting with him as to his prospects of obtaining the nomination. I was about to withdraw, not having
been invited to the apparently private conference, when Bob
asked me to "sit in." I did so, but listened only, until asked
by him what I thought of it. I frankly stated that thus far
I had discovered no apparent demand for his candidacy, that
I thought the efforts as outlined would be in vain; adding
that I feared he would go into the convention with the Wisconsin delegation only, and might not have that entire; that
if he aspired to that high office the way to attain it, in my
opinion, was to make the best record possible in the Senate,
and, "if you please, on the Chautauqua Circuit," where he
had acquired some repute; but that his candidacy at the time
seemed premature and hopeless. At any rate, that was the
substance of my answer. It was the last time I was asked to
"sit in." The result confirmed my forecast. Bob went into
the convention with the Wisconsin delegation, except one delegate from the Wausau district. It may have given him some
advertising. He continued to pursue this ambition with the
same persistence that he had pursued the governorship in the
nineties. I certainly gave him my honest opinion, and feel
now that his burning ambition was unfortunate for himself;

and that if the office had been more modestly sought he might have been more successful. But his impatience would brook no delay. I believe, too, that his service in the Senate might have been more effective for the good of the country, and incidentally better for himself, if he could have forgotten his higher ambition. There was no breach in our friendship because of my failure to give unqualified approval to his candidacy at the time referred to; at any rate, none came to my notice. I have not been able to consider his presidential aspirations otherwise than as unfortunate for himself and for others, as there was at no time a reasonable hope of his success. He met with repeated disappointments, and was a poor loser, as manifested at each repeated defeat. They made him unhappy. When I first knew Bob in Washington, he was a cheerful and happy individual. From his general attitude and expressions in his magazine and elsewhere it is fair to presume that after 1912, and perhaps after 1908, he never voted for the Republican nominee for president.

> Vaulting ambition which o'erleaps itself
> And lands on t'other side.

He became a carping critic of each and every administration. He was entirely unable to do teamwork, which is so necessary in legislation. Perhaps he was better adapted to executive than to legislative service. In legislation, in order to progress at all, there must be compromises. To that necessity La Follette was entirely oblivious. He must have his way, or stop the machine. He, who in old times had aided Tom Reed to break up filibustering in the House, became the greatest obstructionist in the Senate. He had earned his early laurels as an opponent to "boss rule" but became the supreme type of the "boss" in his later years. He made friends easily, but discarded them without a scruple when he thought it to his political advantage. Many of them were good and faithful friends, ready to give him honest advice, but perhaps giving it too disinterestedly; advice that would have served him well in the end. In this manner he estranged many of his early and most loyal friends and earnest supporters; men like Isaac Stephenson, General George E. Bryant, Herman Daley, James Davidson; yes, even his early political foster father, Eli Peterson, did not come up to the mark. Later Senator Lenroot and Governor McGovern were added to the number of cast-off friends; each one sacrificed for no apparent reason, except that La Follette desired more subserviency in his supporters. He is too important a character in Wisconsin history, and his imprint upon its political development was such that discussion of him cannot be omitted. He should be treated fairly, but truthfully, and that I aim to do. There is certainly no one in sight to take his place in the leadership of his clique; believing that term fully justified. But, for the present I would say:

> No farther seek his merits to disclose,
> Or draw his frailties from their dread abode.

MORTGAGE TAXATION

I find from papers kept by me that the so-called mortgage taxation law, advocated by La Follette and enacted in 1903, remained upon the statutes until 1907. In that year I prepared for Governor Davidson a message to the legislature recommending its repeal. The tax commission had in the mean time conducted an extensive investigation of the subject under the direction of Professor Thomas S. Adams, then of the faculty of the economics department of the University of Wisconsin and later a member of the tax commission. The message quoted extensively from his report and showed conclusively the fallacy of any attempt to relieve the debtor by the law as enacted. It stated that the only result of the law thus far had been to exempt the owner of the credit without any corresponding advantage to the borrower; that the interest rate paid by the latter had in fact been increased instead of lowered, as predicted. The message closed as follows: "I therefore recommend that Chapter 378, Laws of 1903, be repealed . . . In restoring the former law the balance of credits above indebtedness which should be assessable and taxable should include moneys as well as credits."

Thus ended the futile effort to reach the interest of the lender. It was a repetition of the experience of California on the same subject. The lender took care of himself by bargaining for a rate of interest sufficiently high to cover any tax he might be required to pay. But he was also protected by the very terms of our mortgages. The income tax later took care of the question, by entirely exempting moneys and credits from taxation as property. It substituted the creditor for the credit; as I had suggested in my dissenting views in 1903.

THE INCOME TAX

The constitutional amendment authorizing an income tax having been ratified by popular vote in 1908, the subject naturally became one of popular discussion. It was an entirely new venture for an American state. It is true that several states had tried it, but with indifferent success. Professor Seligman, of Columbia University, one of the leading economists of the country, had written a bibliography on taxation in Europe, but without particularly dwelling on the merits of the different systems. I read the treatise with care. Professor D. O. Kinsman, of the Whitewater Normal School, when a student at our university, had also written a thesis on attempts at income taxation in the

American colonies and states. He evidently came to the
conclusion that the law had been a failure wherever at-
tempted. He showed, however, that in every instance, the
rate had been so low that the tax became an insignificant
source of revenue, and, having been left to local administration, had not been enforced. My idea of an income tax
was that it should largely replace the personal property
tax; at any rate, that intangibles should be exempted. I
think I may say without undue arrogance that I became the
prime promoter of the tax. Professor Seligman accords me
that distinction in discussing the Wisconsin law. I discussed the principles of the tax in the public press and before public gatherings. In pursuit of information on the
subject, I secured from Richard Guenther, a former colleague in Congress, and then serving as consul at Frank-
fort on the Main, copies of income tax laws in several German states. There was no general income tax for the
German Empire. The states had adopted different revenue
systems and were as free in that respect as our states. I also
secured the laws on the subject from the three Scandinavian
countries.

A peculiarity of the law of Norway was that it granted
exemption on the basis of the number of children and other
dependents, and began by granting exemption for *two*
children, apparently omitting the first one, as if they expected twins to start with. I availed myself of the suggestion and provided exemption for each child under
eighteen. It was the first instance of the kind, I believe, in
income tax legislation in this country. Nor did I find any
such provision in any other European law that came to my
notice. We had before us the income tax law of England.
France had had no income tax. A commission reporting on
the subject about 1905 expressed regret that France had
not availed itself of this system of taxation so generally used

in other leading European countries. This report we had.

I do not recollect that Judge Gilson committed himself on the subject. Mr. Curtiss did not oppose the measure, but remained rather indifferent; thought the movement premature—an old reason for delay.

In Norway a new tax law was passed, I think, in 1908. It provided that the property tax should not exceed seven mills. I can use that designation, as the decimal system prevails there. If the tax rate exceeded that figure it should gradually be lowered. If less, it might be raised to that figure. There was no arbitrary limit to the income tax rate. Occasionally the Norwegian press here refers to local tax rates in Norway; and sometimes they are as high as twenty-five per cent. In other words, the property tax rate was stationary, and the income rate flexible; the reverse of our system. The local unit determined the rate, as it does the property rate here.

When the legislature of 1909 convened it was my duty to prepare the bill. This I did. As far as possible I followed the federal law of 1893, especially in the definitions of income. Coming up from Chicago one evening I talked the matter over with Professor Richard T. Ely, then of the economics department of our University, and recognized as one of the country's leading economists. I told him in a general way what I was trying to do. He informed me that before coming to Wisconsin, while connected with Johns Hopkins University, he had drafted a bill on the subject for the legislature of Maryland, and that we seemed to be fairly agreed as to the general plan. Coming from so distinguished a source, this was certainly encouraging. I had attended his "seminary" meetings of his students and interested outsiders which were generally held in the evening at his residence. He had expressed approval of my views on exemption of credits, and I had read my full report to the seminary.

Mr. Ingram, of Durand, asked me to let him have the bill so that he could introduce it in the assembly. I hurried its preparation. A couple of days later Senator Paul O. Husting, of Mayville, Dodge County, made the same request. A few changes were made, but the two bills were substantially the same, and were introduced in the two houses on the same day, February 25. After some time a public hearing was had in the assembly chamber, where I was the principal advocate of the measure, for which I by no means claimed perfection. The Merchants and Manufacturers Association of the state was opposed to it and was represented by Professor Kinsman, referred to above. The bill went further as to rates in the higher brackets than does the present law. In fact, as an income tax our rates are very moderate. On this subject I may allude to a meeting I had in Appleton after the enactment of the law. A leading banker of that city rose and wished to ask me questions. He stated that he had a ten thousand dollar bond drawing six per cent interest, and asked whether I considered it fair that he should pay a tax on that income. This was the very best question for an illustration. I told him that under the former law his bond was assessable as property at its true value, which was presumably $10,000; that the tax rate that year in his city was two per cent, which would make his tax $200.00; that the income from his bond, being $600.00, would at the highest rate of 6 per cent subject him to a tax of $36.00. Which did he prefer to pay, a property tax of $200.00 or an income tax of $36.00? No further questions came from that source. Chances were, of course, that, as in most such cases, the bond had not been assessed; and a grin from the audience seemed to recognize that fact. I had in my draft provided for a rate of twenty per cent on incomes in excess of $160,000, working up gradually to that high level. I wanted some margin for the supporters of the bill to trade on, not expecting that rate to remain. But even the rate of twenty per cent on the income of the bond referred to would amount to only $120.00, and my questioner would still be the gainer by $80.00.

The session of 1909 did not take final action on the income tax. Before it adjourned June 15 an interim committee was appointed to make further investigation, hold hearings, etc., with instructions to report to the next session. The senate members were Marsh, Kleczka, and Hazelwood; the assembly members, Georgi, McConnell, Ingram, and Towers.

NEW TAX COMMISSIONERS

Before taking up the report of the special legislative committee it seems proper to refer to changes made in the personnel of the commission. Judge Gilson had been reappointed by Governor Davidson when his term expired in 1909, and had continued as chairman. Mr. Curtiss' term would expire May, 1911. Francis E. McGovern was elected governor in 1910, taking office the following January. He had been an early and consistent "Progressive," and had served with distinction as district attorney of Milwaukee County; had, in fact, been elected to that office the last time as an independent candidate, thus showing unusual strength. He was a graduate of the University of Wisconsin and had great respect for its faculty. He had set his heart on appointing Professor Adams, alluded to above, to the place occupied by Mr. Curtiss. I thought the latter entitled to reappointment, but the Governor thought that an economist should have the place. In the meantime, Judge Gilson resigned; perhaps out of friendship to Curtiss, thinking that by so doing he would secure his continuance in the service. Mr. Adams was appointed, and proved an efficient and practical member of the commission. Mr. Thomas E. Lyons of Superior, a leading attorney of that city and an old friend of McGovern from university days, was appointed to succeed Gilson. The commission was thus reorganized and I was elected chairman, which position I held until May 1, 1921. Both my new colleagues worked harmoniously with me in support of the income tax. Our relations were pleasant and agreeable throughout. Adams was more of an expert at accountancy than Lyons or myself, and was of great service in the inauguration of the income tax, especially in formulating the reports to be submitted, and later in editing the returns. But this is ahead of the story.

INCOME TAX LAW CONTINUED

The special committee made its report to the legislature of 1911, recommending passage. The bill had been amended in several respects; undoubtedly improved in some parts, but not in all. A public hearing, largely attended, took place January 27 in the assembly chamber, with the three commissioners present. Two material changes were proposed to which we especially objected; also some minor ones. The first related to the definition of the word "person" in the first part of the bill. The committee's report read: "The term 'person' as used in this act shall mean and include any individual, firm, copartnership," etc., . . . "organized for profit and having a capital stock represented by shares, etc."

To this I said: "Whoever heard of an individual organized for profit and represented by capital stock?" That was the end of that amendment. Another more serious change provided that the rate of taxation for the income of corporations should be based upon the relation which the net income bore to the assessed valuation of the property, varying the rate up to fifteen per cent. I never discovered where this suggestion came from; except that in the law of Sweden there was a somewhat similar provision. All the commissioners found this provision impractical in administration, and after considerable difficulty secured a change. It is likely that in Sweden the embarrassment of interstate operations would not present the difficulties that obtain here.

THE PERSONAL PROPERTY TAX OFFSET

This provision was evidently borrowed from the law of British Columbia, which simply provided that where the taxpayer was subject to an income tax and also to a personal property tax, he should pay the higher tax. This is really simpler than our law, which provided that under such circumstances the tax on the personal property may be offset against the income tax.

The bill as prepared by me provided for the exemption of practically all personal property. As the income naturally falls upon merchants and manufacturers, those interests certainly stood in their own light if they assisted in securing the offset provision. In 1927 the legislature, by merely repealing this provision, restored both taxes. The personal property tax had been notoriously badly administered both as to inequalities and omissions in the assessments, and these were largely the ills that the income tax was intended to remedy. It is true that in 1911 the legislature could not foresee the yield of the new tax and sought a safeguard by retaining the old tax as well. Railroads and some other corporations paying taxes directly into the state treasury were exempted from the income tax, and remained so. Moneys and credits, household goods and furnishings, etc., were exempted. As to the prospective yield of the tax I find myself quoted in the proceedings of the National Tax Association at its meeting in Des Moines in 1912, while our first assessment was still in the making. I said that the year 1911 was hardly a normal year, "still we expect to get approximately $3,000,000 in taxes from incomes." The final assessment for that year showed that the income tax amounted to $3,501,161. In this address I discussed the law at length, both as to its principles and its history.

How the law struck outsiders at the time is best illustrated by remarks of Professor Bullock of Harvard, who said, at the end of my address: "It seems to me worth while to call attention to the truly remarkable character of the report that the gentleman from Wisconsin has just made upon the working of the Wisconsin income tax. Up to the time of the enactment of that income tax, there were very few students of taxation in this country who were not convinced that no state could hope to administer satisfactorily a tax upon incomes. I have said that myself in print, but that was a dozen years ago; and I am glad to say that I have changed my opinion on that point and also put that into print, two or three years before the Wisconsin tax was enacted. Apparently students of taxation must, at least with regard to Wisconsin, revise all their ideas in regard to the impossibility of a state administering with reasonable success a tax upon incomes.

"In regard to the question asked a moment ago in regard to the means of knowing whether or not full returns of income were secured in Wisconsin, Mr. Haugen might very well have added what the head of the income tax department of Wisconsin told me last spring, that after conferring with people about their income tax returns he was not only satisfied that in the main in the overwhelming majority of cases they were given honest returns, but was also satisfied that the people on the whole were making them pretty cheerfully,

with a sense of relief and satisfaction that they had at last
got a tax law under which they could make honest returns.
Now the statement is a remarkable one, because it is a statement of the first consistent attempt made in this country to
carry through a comprehensive reform of personal property
taxation.   Other states by enacting three-mill tax laws or by
registration taxes or one thing or another, have improved the
details of their system, and may be working by such methods
and classification towards something that will ultimately be
a systematic solution of the tax problem along the line of a
property tax; but here is the most comprehensive and systematic attempt yet made, and apparently with success.

"The third point I wish to make has been made by Mr.
Adams of the Wisconsin commission already, namely, that
here we have the first attempt on American soil to carry out
the taxation of either property or income by means of assessors responsible directly to state control and free from
local influence."

I have quoted Dr. Bullock thus at length because he is
recognized as a leader among economists in general and on
the subject of taxation in particular.   He has been a regular
attendant on the meetings of the National Tax Association
and has served as its president.   I may add here that at his
suggestion I was invited in the winter of 1917, to address a
committee of the legislature of Massachusetts on the subject
of income taxation—my only visit to New England.

THE NATIONAL TAX ASSOCIATION

I became a member of this organization at its birth, although not present at its organization in Indianapolis in
1907.   I had attended conferences of tax men before; the
first one in 1901 in Buffalo, New York.   After the organization of the association I was present at most of its annual
conferences as long as I remained on the Wisconsin Com-

mission, was elected its president at Chicago in 1919, and served as such at its meeting in Salt Lake City in 1920. I succeeded Professor Bullock.

The Association conducts no propaganda. It has proved a serviceable organization. Its object is: "To formulate and announce . . . the best informed economic thought and administrative experience for the correct guidance of public opinion, and legislative and administrative action on all questions pertaining to taxation, and to interstate and international comity in taxation." It is thus purely educational. It has no hobby. In a general way it may be said that the activities of the Wisconsin commission in its several aspects had its sincere approval and support, our most important venture being the income tax.

TAX COMMISSION

The county boards had in the early part of the La Follette administration, been authorized to appoint a supervisor of assessments for each county. After the enactment of the income tax law, the law on this subject was repealed and the commission was given authority to appoint income tax assessors. These officials were clad with the powers and duties formerly possessed by the appointees of the county boards. Under the later law the commission was authorized to join two or more counties together under the supervision of one assessor of incomes. These officials have been of great service in securing better observances of the law by local assessors. Where the former officials had rendered efficient service, the commission generally appointed them to the new positions. No attention was paid to partisanship in these selections.

I appeared before the assembly committee on taxation when these matters came up. A Democratic member of the committee said: "But you have not appointed any

Democrats." I said, "We appointed John Ross in Waukesha. Don't you call him a Democrat? And we appointed Tom Cleary of Grant. What do you call him?" These men had been leading members of their party in their respective communities. A Socialist from Milwaukee said: "But you have appointed no Socialist." To this I was able to respond: "We appointed Mr. Storch of Taylor County. Don't you recognize him as a Socialist?" That seemed satisfactory. I might have added Charles Staples of Polk, approved Socialist. They were all appointed under civil service rules, and all made good.

After the election of local assessors in the spring, meetings of assessors were held in each county, and as far as we were able to attend, one of the commissioners was present. That had been the requirement before the income tax. Judge Gilson was reluctant about attending these conferences; so that duty fell largely to Mr. Curtiss and myself. In this way we visited nearly every county in the state and came into closer touch with the assessors and their local difficulties. I may say that I have been in every county in the state, and in most of them a number of times; have seen the virgin timber in its original luxuriance, and the land in its denuded state. I was going up through Marinette and Florence counties one day on the Wisconsin and Michigan Railroad. I was talking with a lumberman when we were about on the line between the two counties, and looking out on the desert, he asked me what I thought that land was worth. It looked like a sandy barren waste, and I said fifty cents an acre would seem a high price. He said: "Ike Stephenson's son-in-law sold this land last winter to parties from Indiana for ten dollars an acre." Evidently he took advantage of a good covering of snow. There is some good land in Northern Wisconsin; but there is much that it is a crime to sell for farming purposes. I have had some doubt

as to the propriety of the State's joining in soliciting settlers
to go into that part of the state. Not that settlement should
be discouraged; but let individuals act upon their own responsibility and judgment. It is still to be demonstrated
whether reforestation can be introduced in a practical way
without too great expense to the public. Fires are unquestionably the great difficulty to overcome. Whether under-
taken by the federal or state government, the utmost care
must be taken, as it would undoubtedly appear that lands
now returned delinquent for nonpayment of taxes would
immediately be represented as of great value. I do not
question the desirability of reforestation, but believe the
public should be protected against too severe bleeding. Many
of the hillsides of the Mississippi and its tributaries ought not
to be overlooked. They used to have good white pine; the
soil is good, and would, if fires are prevented and young
trees planted, be even more inviting a field than the sandy
areas in the north. There is no more beautiful tree than
our native white pine. But it takes time and patience—a
generation, no doubt—for the first harvest. I first visited
the Superior region in 1877 attending court with Judge
Barron in "Old Superior" (there was no West Superior
then) and in Bayfield and Ashland.

A little incident occurred when the jury was drawn in
Bayfield. A justice of the peace, a Mr. Bell, residing on
Madeline Island, was drawn on the jury. He claimed exemption because of his official position. The judge overruled him. Mr. Bell said that he would waive the question
and serve, "But there may be a difference of *judicature* on
that point." As justice of the peace, it was told, he had
granted divorces. But he was not the only J. P. who had
assumed that authority. That also occurred in Prescott,
Pierce County, where the parties later appeared in the circuit court with their difficulties.

CHAPTER VII

Under McGovern and Philipps and in Montana

Davidson's administration went on smoothly and satisfactorily. He was affable and desired to serve the public, not forgetting his friends. Late one Saturday evening the Madison Street Railway Company started to place poles for the support of their electric wire on the capitol side of the streets about the capitol square. Going up towards the capitol on Sunday morning the governor joined me, and stated his difficulty. He said he had appealed to the attorney general for advice and had been told that he could not get out an injunction on Sunday. I immediately answered: "You do not need an injunction. It is your duty to protect the property of the State. Call out your capitol police; if that is not enough call on the adjutant general. Don't bother with the attorney general." That appealed to Jim, and the work was suspended. Why the attorney general did not acquaint him with the power he possessed without resorting to an injunction, I could not understand. It was reported that the governor said to the representative of the railway company, who interviewed him at the capitol, that if the company proceeded with their plans he would call out the militia to stop them.

A persistent effort was made by cities with lake harbors to have so much of the railroad tax returned to them as would fairly represent the value of the elevators used in transferring grain and other products from railway to lake vessels. This had been consistently opposed by the tax commission, as an undue favor to such cities. A bill was, however, passed and presented to the governor, and he was in

distress as to what to do with it. His private secretary, Col.
O. G. Munson, came to me about it. We conferred with
the other members of the commission, but they thought our
advice would be of no avail. Mr. Munson disagreed and
asked me to prepare a veto message for the governor. This
I did. I think I found some legal authority in the courts
of other states sustaining our contention, and quoted them.
At any rate, my opinion had the approval of my colleagues.
The message was laid before the governor. He read it and
approved, but was afraid of the political effect, especially
in Superior. I had about given up hope and was ready to
leave him, when Munson motioned me to remain. This I
did, and saw the governor's signature affixed to the veto.
Later a like bill was signed, but it was held invalid by the
supreme court, thus sustaining the commission and the governor. Later, however, another bill, with changes to obviate
the legal difficulties, was again introduced and passed, and
it remains the law today.

Appointments are always troublesome to the appointing
powers. A vacancy occurred in the supreme court, and Robert M. Bashford, a leading Madison attorney, became an
aspirant. He had the nominal, though apparently not the
cordial support of his brethren of the Madison bar. Mr.
Davidson consulted me in the matter, but said he would have
to appoint Bashford, or it would be uncomfortable for
him to live in Madison. I told him that in my opinion Bashford would not be elected at the succeeding spring election.
I suggested that he appoint one of the circuit judges. That
seemed the natural and consistent thing to do, and I suggested Judge Vinje of the Superior circuit, whom I knew
personally, before whom I had practised to some extent,
and who had made a good record on the bench. But the
pressure for Bashford was too strong. He was appointed,
but was defeated by John Barnes when he came up for re-

ëlection in the spring of 1908. With others, I had encouraged Barnes to enter the race.

John Barnes had served as a member of the railroad commission, but had resigned in 1907 when the legislature passed an act, contrary to the advice of that commission, fixing the maximum passenger rates on the leading railroads of the state at two cents a mile. The commission had fixed such rate at two and one-half cents a mile, giving its reasons, and had asked the governor to veto the bill as passed. My recollection is that in New York the governor had vetoed a similar bill. Since the passenger traffic of New York was much heavier that was quoted to the governor as a fair precedent to follow. But he signed it, and Mr. Barnes resigned in protest. He had rendered good service on the commission, and the action of the legislature could hardly be considered a personal reflection on him or his colleagues. He was a valuable member of the supreme court, but after a few years resigned to take up the practice of law as counsel for the Northwestern Life Insurance Company, in Milwaukee, finding that more lucrative.

Judge Dodge of the supreme court resigned early in September, 1910. La Follette called one afternoon, told me of the resignation, and asked whether I could reach Davidson in regard to the appointment of a successor. I said that I was going to Milwaukee the next morning to attend the annual meeting of the National Tax Association; that Davidson was going in to extend the welcome of the state to the Association; that I had helped him to prepare the welcoming speech, which I had in my pocket; that I would very likely be in touch with him. I also told him that I had suggested Judge Vinje in regard to a former appointment. That seemed satisfactory to Bob. There was no question as to Governor Davidson's friendly attitude toward Vinje. He probably regretted his former appointment of Bashford.

Vinje was appointed and is now occupying the distinguished position of chief justice, having been promoted to that position, in the natural course of events, as the oldest judge in service on the death of Judge Siebecker, brother-in-law of La Follette.[3]

I may mention in this connection, that during our service together in Congress, and while Hoard was governor, Bob asked me to join in recommending Siebecker, then his law partner, to Governor Hoard for the circuit judgeship of Dane County. A vacancy had occurred in that office, I think through the death of the incumbent. This I did, and the appointment was made. Later, while on the tax commission, I again joined in recommending Judge Siebecker for a position on the supreme bench, as successor to Judge Bardeen in 1903. La Follette was then governor, but thought it wise and prudent to have the approval of members of the bar, and such approval Judge Siebecker had.

MC GOVERN ADMINISTRATION

Francis E. McGovern succeeded Davidson January, 1911. He had elements of strength not possessed by his predecessor. This can be said without reflecting in the least on Davidson, whose administration was clean and above reproach. But McGovern had the advantage of a classical and legal education followed by years of legal practice at the bar. Add to this a level head, good judgment and clearness of vision, together with absolute independence of political entanglements, and I believe it can fairly be said that he ranks with the very best of our chief magistrates. The income tax had been approved by the people, and in the election of 1910 the Democratic platform endorsed it, as did the Republican. But in the campaign of 1912 the Demo-

[3] While these notes were being prepared Judge Vinje died, March 23, 1929. He had rendered valuable service to the people of the state.

cratic platform viciously denounced the income tax law. The Democratic candidate, J. G. Karel, had declared against it before the primary in September. On this subject I find myself quoted in my address at the Des Moines meeting of the Tax Association, before referred to. It happened to be on the day following the primary election. I said:

> The situation in Wisconsin is somewhat peculiar today. I read in the papers this morning that the candidate for Democratic nomination for governor, who was running on an anti-income tax platform, won out yesterday. The Republican candidate nominated is in favor of the law with such amendments as may prove to be necessary and which will be presented at the coming session of the legislature. So we have, as it seems now, a good, clean-cut, economic issue before the people of the state of Wisconsin this fall; an issue as to whether the system of taxation which we have had heretofore shall again be introduced, or whether we shall develop the theory of the income tax law. And I believe it is rather fortunate that the issue is squarely made and that an issue so clean can be presented by each party to the people during the present campaign and be discussed throughout the state, because it will give them information not only as to this law but as to the operations of the law as we have had it heretofore. The people of the state ought to have the benefit of a thorough discussion of economic questions of that kind.

Mr. McGovern was elected by something over twelve thousand plurality, and that in spite of defection in his own party which will be referred to later. He undoubtedly aided materially in clearing up the situation on the tax question. It may be too, that this issue assisted in securing his own election.

At this time we had in Madison what was known as "The Saturday Lunch Club." It was an open forum, attended by state officers and employees at the capitol, university professors, and any business men or outsiders who felt interested in the subjects for discussion. Governor McGovern took an active part in these meetings, and was always clear, logical, and to the point. It was said of him that he never split an infinitive. He certainly showed a trained mind, well balanced and logical, a consistent "progressive" in every respect. He had been a regular supporter of the La Follette program. I know of no criticism of any of his official acts. His record certainly will stand comparison with that of the very best of our governors.

I have referred to the McKinley Bill as being the principal cause of the defeat of the Republican party in Wisconsin in 1890. The "Treasury Cases" undoubtedly contributed. The state treasurers had been in the habit—at least some of them had—of pocketing the interest collected from state deposits in banks. Senator Sawyer was the principal responsible bondsman. The Peck administration had brought action to collect from the ex-treasurers and their bondsmen. This led to the conflict between Senator Sawyer and La Follette heretofore referred to. The Peck administration, however, laid itself open to a charge of which the Republicans did not fail to take advantage. Some of the officials and employees of the capitol had become interested in printing contracts to which the state was a party. It was charged that they had failed to let the printing to the lowest bidder, as provided by law. This resulted in what became known as the "Roster Case," which was tried before Judge Siebecker in the circuit court at Madison, resulting adversely to the Democratic administration, and undoubtedly contributing to the defeat of that party in 1894. During McGovern's first term a somewhat similar matter presented itself. The *Wisconsin State Journal* was owned and edited by Richard Lloyd Jones. Like many another able journalist, he was not rolling in wealth. He was a loyal supporter of the administration. A proposition was advanced to form a corporation to become the owner of the paper, and state officers and others in the capitol were invited to become stockholders. The proposition seemed plausible and inviting. A meeting was held, the matter was discussed and adjourned for final action at a later date. Governor McGovern, Judge Siebecker, and others from the capitol participated, including myself. Thinking the matter over, it occurred to me that this might become another "Roster Case," and on the morning of the adjournment day I called on Judge Siebecker, then on the supreme court bench, and asked him if there was any difference between this proposition and the "Roster Case." He immediately responded: "This matter has worried me all night, and I am glad you came in. I tried the 'Roster Case' in the circuit court and I can see no difference." We concluded that we would withdraw. Asked if I had seen the governor, I replied that I was going to his office next, "but I thought I better see you first." He said I might give his views. I saw McGovern and he immediately concurred in our decision to keep out, and authorized me so to tell the meeting. He attended in person, however, and when one of the participants suggested that it was too late to withdraw, he said: "Better withdraw now than get knocked out later." There was no hesitancy on his part any more than on the judge's. So the proposition went by the board. There was no aftermath.

La Follette was a candidate for senator and McGovern for governor in the campaign of 1910 and the relations between them were mutually friendly and harmonious.

NATIONAL CONVENTION 1912

An unexpected breach in the relations of these distinguished citizens of the state grew out of the national Republican convention in Chicago in 1912. I was not present at the convention. La Follette had again announced his candidacy, I believe against the better judgment of some of his best friends. He had during the preceding winter addressed a meeting of newspaper men in Philadelphia at a publishers' dinner and had broken down physically and mentally during his address. Such seemed to be the universal opinion of the press at the time. The facts were certainly important as bearing on his campaign, although in his autobiography he speaks of the event as of trifling consequence, explaining that he was slightly indisposed. The press reported that in delivering the text of his manuscript, which might normally have occupied little more than thirty minutes, he took the floor at eleven o'clock and continued to speak until nearly two in the morning, repeating the same matter over and over until most of his auditors had left the hall. Those nearest to him advised his withdrawal the next day; and to this he seems at first to have consented. But other advisers, together with his insatiable ambition, prevailed, and in a few days he was again in the field.

The length of his political speeches was an old weakness of La Follette's and he had repeatedly been told so by his best friends, even when governor. A little incident comes to mind here. Mrs. La Follette was making an outdoor political address on Johnson Street near our home one evening, along about 1907 or 1908. Mrs. Haugen attended, and at the close of the meeting invited Mrs. La Follette and other ladies up to the house for a cup of coffee. Mrs. Joseph Jastrow was of the party. Talking with the ladies, I said: "Mrs. La Follette, I understand that you talk just as well as Bob does." Mrs. Jastrow added: "Yes, and she talks just as long." Mrs. La Follette took the joke good-naturedly and laughed with the rest.

Wisconsin sent a solid La Follette delegation to the Chicago convention in 1912, headed by Governor McGovern. The delegates met for conference and it seems that they unanimously agreed to support McGovern for temporary chairman of the convention; and that action was publicly announced. Elihu Root was the choice of the Taft supporters for the position. It has been a source of dispute among the delegates as to the cause of the rupture in our state delegation. These facts, however, seem beyond question. No candidate had a majority of delegates whose title to seats was unquestioned. Taft had the support of seventy-eight delegates from the South whose election was challenged before the committee on credentials. The Roosevelt and La Follette delegates could, by combining, prevent the organization of the Taft forces, and it was agreed by the Roosevelt men that they would support McGovern for the position.

The only way to defeat Taft was to defeat the election of Root, and McGovern and his supporters took the position that delegates whose titles were in dispute had no vote in the convention until their right to seats had been determined. This was certainly logical. A record of undisputed delegates which I have before me, shows the uncontested votes as follows: Taft 480; Roosevelt 502; La Follette 36; and Cummins 10. La Follette was certainly a poor third in the running and it must always remain questionable, even with the union of the anti-Taft forces, whether a sufficient number of Roosevelt delegates could have been brought over to nominate him. But it seems beyond question that the only way to defeat Taft's nomination was the one suggested by the supporters of McGovern. When it came to a vote some of the La Follette men deserted McGovern and voted for Root. Result, the nomination of Taft on the first ballot. And his defeat at the election.

In his magazine and elsewhere La Follette accused McGovern of being a traitor to his cause. I have seen no good reason for his friends' change of position as to the temporary chairmanship during the convention. McGovern naturally resented the charge of disloyalty, in the press and elsewhere. The national convention was held in June. It seems that after some weeks La Follette regretted the controversy which he had started. I am reminded of the fact that Judge Siebecker came to me and stated that if McGovern would stop any further discussion in the press La Follette would desist; and he asked me to see the governor and tell him. No doubt the judge thought the controversy unfortunate and was solicitous for harmony between the two. I carried the message to McGovern. He readily assented, stating that he had not begun it but was forced into it in self defense. An armistice of several weeks followed. But when Roosevelt announced his candidacy in the latter part of August as the "Progressive" candidate for the presidency on an independent ticket, and McGovern announced his support of him, all former charges and some new ones were let loose. Bob was determined to be the only dyed-in-the-wool leader of "Progressivism." In the language attributed by a local wit to a candidate for mayor of Superior,

> There may be other pebbles on the beach
> But I am the only real pictured rock.

Taft had visited Madison some years earlier, I think during the early part of the 1908 campaign, and in a speech which I heard had expressed his regret that Senator Spooner had withdrawn from public service. He lauded him as a very able legislator. That in itself was enough to antagonize Bob, but added to this was his own defeat in the convention of that year. His renewed war on McGovern, however, resulted when the latter announced his support of Roosevelt. The campaign went on; if there was any pronounced support of McGovern by La Follette I am not cognizant of it. But this I remember. La Follette addressed a large meeting in the University gymnasium; towards the end of his address he advised the support of the state ticket, but added, "As to McGovern, we will attend to him later." Not a very cordial recommendation of the head of the state ticket! There was some applause; but I mentally resented it.

I had been in the habit of contributing to the Republican campaign fund, and had made a modest contribution in support of the La Follette delegate ticket in the spring election; had also promised one of Bob's close Madison friends a contribution to the campaign fund in the fall. One evening, shortly after the gymnasium speech referred to, I was called up by telephone, the voice stating: "Haugen, we need some money; can you let us have some tomorrow?" I said: "How is this money to be used? For McGovern, or against him?" No answer. I added: "You don't expect me to contribute to the defeat of the Republican candidate for governor, do you?" No answer. The receivers were hung up. A few mornings later I was in the state treasurer's office when Senator Scott of Barron came in. He was an ardent La Follette supporter and I think had been a delegate to the national convention. He was also chairman of the Republican state committee. He showed us a check just handed him by the governor. I said to myself, if McGovern gives Scott a check, I will, and then and there made my contribution. McGovern was elected.

The legislature met at the usual date in January, 1913. Then came the "sequel" which I mentioned in a former article, when I said that I made no contributions to the campaign fund after 1912; also the carrying out of the threat to attend to McGovern later. Almost immediately after the organization of the legislature a committee was appointed, with Scott as chairman, to look into the political activities of the personnel in the capitol. I had never heard of any criticism on that account while La Follette was governor, or, for that matter, later. I was asked to come up to the senate chamber, and of course complied. Some informal discussion took place, and with a somewhat sanctimonious air the chairman said that perhaps all departments had better be investigated. I was sworn as the first witness, but the lunch hour having arrived, the committee took a recess to a later hour, when I was asked to be present for examination.

I went down to my office and dug out the check which I had contributed to the La Follette campaign in the spring;

also the check given Scott, and with these in my vest pocket presented myself at the designated hour. It was well known that I had supported McGovern throughout the campaign, without being an active campaigner. I was ready to take the stand. But as a preliminary I was called aside by the then lieutenant governor, who said: "Now you understand, Haugen, that what we want is what is against McGovern." I think I have his exact words. To this I promptly answered: "Tom, I was sworn to tell the whole truth, and I am going to begin with the contribution I made to the La Follette campaign last spring." I was not placed on the stand and the investigation ended before it commenced. I broke it up. When I left the chamber a couple of newspaper men accosted me and asked what had happened. Reply, "I just threw the monkey wrench into the cylinder." Thus ended the hypocritical effort to reach the governor only, without blacking their own fingers. It also ended my campaign contributions; not that I had been a heavy contributor, but in every campaign something was given. And there had never been any modesty or hesitancy in soliciting aid, not only during campaigns, but also to build up the *La Follette Magazine*. For the latter purpose I twice contributed small amounts to put agents in the field to get subscribers.

I cannot say that I ever came to a personal break with La Follette, but when "Fighting Bob" became the "Fighting Pacifist" and continued his attacks on the government and its allies after we entered the conflict, not only in speech but every week in his magazine, I could not endure it any longer. I sent notice to the paper to stop sending it to me, saying that I did not want it in the house. That was no doubt an unforgivable sin.

The natural course for the Progressives to have pursued in 1912 would seem to have been to support Roosevelt, he having the largest following. He might have been elected, and probably would have been. With his positive character he might have swung the "big stick" early in the conflict, and made the Kaiser hesitate. He might even have been "delighted" to do so. If he had thus stopped the war at its very beginning, it is reasonable to imagine that he would have called down upon his head denunciations for interfering in European affairs, and that by the very same men who denounced our entering the war at a very late date. Roosevelt would have caught it coming or going.

Mr. Hambro, president of the Norwegian *Storting* and editor of *Morgenbladet,* a leading newspaper in Oslo (Christiania), recently published the following anent Roosevelt, which may be news in this country. Roosevelt was returning from his African hunting trip, had visited the Kaiser, and was on his way to Oslo. A delegation, including Mr. Hambro, met him at the Swedish border to escort him to the capital. He talked freely with the newspaper men, and told about his visit with the Kaiser. He said he had remarked to him that with his splendid military establishment he might easily capture Belgium. The Kaiser said that had occurred to him. Then Roosevelt turned to the newspaper men and said: "Don't you tell any of this. If you do, I will say it is a newspaper lie."

There was one matter in Roosevelt's record that I have never been able to justify in my own mind, and that is the manner in which he took Panama. In a speech in Madison he boastingly said, "I took Panama." I have always felt that recognizing the rebellion in Panama the day following the outbreak had too much the appearance of having connived at it in advance. And having a war vessel at the place to support the movement against a friendly nation does not lessen the suspicion. We certainly needed the canal, and it would seem that it might have been acquired by friendly negotiation, even if at a higher price; but it would have avoided the unfriendly feeling on the part of Spanish America which Roosevelt's precipitate action undoubtedly caused. It is the manner in which he "took" it, and not the taking.

The unfortunate break between La Follette and Mc-Govern resulted in defeating the latter in a subsequent election for the senatorship, where he would have been an honor and credit to the state; and deprived Wisconsin of his eminent qualifications as a public servant.

GOVERNOR PHILIPP

Emanuel L. Philipp succeeded McGovern as governor in January, 1915, and served six years. He was a level-headed business man; gave the state the benefit of his good judgment, and left a creditable record; did not seem to have any other or further political ambition. He was fair and impartial and ready to yield his preconceived ideas when convinced that he was in error. In the campaign he had suggested that he would reorganize the public service by abolishing some of the bureaus and changing some commissions by reducing them to one-man commissions. Among the latter was the tax commission. During the session of the legislature a meeting with the committee on taxation was called in the governor's office. I attended on behalf of the commission. The matter came up. Philipp had suggested, among other things, that the administration of the income tax might be left to local officials. To this I said that such had been the effort in some other states, where the income tax had admittedly been a failure for that reason, while in Wisconsin its success was largely due to its centralized administration; that imposing upon one man the duty of assessing railroads with valuations running into hundreds of millions, would be a hazardous undertaking for the individual; that he would be subjected to criticism of partiality to the corporations, or accused of playing the demagogue in over-assessing them; that the same would be true in regard to the income tax, where all the corporations in the state subject to it are assessable directly by the commission.

Before the hearing closed the governor said with absolute frankness and without the least hesitation: "Mr. Haugen, I guess that plan would not work." I could but admire him for his readiness to abandon his former views, and that seemed to be his attitude throughout his administration. He had been considered a "stalwart" and a retrogressive during the campaign. He left no evidence of that character in his service. He was public spirited.

I had been reappointed by Governor McGovern in 1913 for an eight year term. Prof. T. S. Adams resigned from the commission in 1915 to join the faculty of Yale University, Mr. Lyons and I both regretted his departure. He evidently found university work more to his taste than making assessments and pondering on income tax returns. In those days the commissioners themselves did most of the auditing of the corporation returns. The two commissioners were naturally concerned as to Adams' successor. Mr. Carroll Atwood had been appointed assessor of incomes for Milwaukee County, and had made a splendid record in the most important county of the state. He had appointed John Leenhouts as assistant. The two had worked together in harmony, and the latter is entitled to a share in the success attained. Mr. Lyons and I joined in recommending Mr. Atwood to the vacancy in the commission, giving our reasons for the choice, and adding that it seemed entirely proper to recognize Milwaukee with its one-fifth of the valuation of the entire state, and pointing out that it had never had a member on the permanent commission. Governor Philipp readily agreed with us and appointed Mr. Atwood, whose companionship I enjoyed to the end of my term in 1921.

I am not aware that Governor McGovern or Governor Philipp at any time drew upon anyone connected with the commission for any political work or assistance. My own contribution to the campaign fund was entirely voluntary.

After our entry into the World War the personnel in the capitol, in evidence of their loyalty, organized to raise money through the sale of Liberty Bonds. I was one of the solicitors and I think we were reasonably successful. I do not remember that I encountered one instance where the individual approached did not willingly respond according to his means. Mr. Lyons and I each carried ten thousand dollars, or two years' salary, and I borrowed money to do so. After the close of the war I sold the bonds at about ninety-three or ninety-four. I was under the military age during the Civil War, and over age when the Spanish War came on. My fever for the service was probably greater during the Civil War, when I was a boy of fifteen, than at any later period; so many of my acquaintances had gone South; and many of them remained there. But that was not a deterrent to a boy of that age.

Some of our belligerent pacifists in Wisconsin supported President Wilson openly in 1916, because "he kept us out of the war." Hughes, however, carried the state, but by a reduced plurality. But Wilson was reëlected, and early in his second term was forced into the war. La Follette had had his own political fences to look after in 1916, and was elected by a good majority.

My service on the tax commission had been pleasant and congenial. Acquaintances had been formed and friendships established, which are pleasant remembrances. I feel that I had the good will of the office force and that it remains, but I knew the end of my Wisconsin service was at hand, and I was preparing for it. I did not look for further public service, but something turned up unexpectedly.

SERVICE IN MONTANA

About the middle of April I had a telephone call from Governor McGovern inquiring whether I would be free to go to Montana as assistant or adviser to the Board of Equalization of that state. The inquiry had come from the governor, Joseph M. Dixon. I said I expected to be free after May first. Within a few days a letter was received from Governor Dixon, and after some correspondence I accepted the position, which no doubt came to me because of my connection with the National Tax Association, of which I had been president the previous year. Other friends besides McGovern sent their recommendations. The office force had prepared me for my exit by presenting me with a splendid traveling bag as a souvenir of our separation. Cordial relations had been formed between Governor McGovern and Governor Dixon in 1912, when Dixon, then senator, was the campaign manager of the Roosevelt Progressive campaign, of which our governor became an ardent supporter. These men had much in common, and were fearless adherents to the cause they espoused, without any ulterior personal motives.

Governor Dixon met me cordially, and introduced me to his colleagues on the board, of which he, as governor, was the chairman. The other members were the attorney general, secretary of state, state treasurer, and state auditor, all elective officers whose primary duties had no relation to tax questions, which necessarily became a secondary matter. The situation was strange and necessarily unfamiliar. The board was created by the constitution. Its duties were broad and many, not unlike those possessed by our tax commission. It fixed the property assessments and the tax, supplemented with license taxes on some industries.

Senator Clark, the copper king, was the president of their constitutional convention in 1889, and had not failed

to protect the mining industry. The constitution provided
that mineral in the ground was not to be considered in assessing real estate; that the surface value only must be the
base for the assessment, no matter at what price land containing mineral was sold. There had, in fact, been no real
equalization between counties; nor between the general property and railroads and other corporations assessed directly
by the board. As to state assessments, the situation was the
same as in Wisconsin under our old state board of assessment. The difficulty on my advent in Montana was that,
as in the country generally, real estate had suffered a serious
deflation after the close of the war. In Wisconsin the high
year in real estate was 1919, and that seemed true throughout the Northwest and West.

On my arrival Governor Dixon suggested that I take
up my residence in that state; that a tax commission was
likely to be created by the next session of the legislature,
and that he would make me chairman of such commission.
I said that I was too old to give up my citizenship in Wisconsin, although I highly appreciated his good will. I also
felt, without expressing it, that ambitious old settlers and
aspiring politicians might object to the appointment of a
new arrival and "interloper" to so important and fairly lucrative a position.

After assisting in the railroad assessments I was forced
to return to Wisconsin because of my health. This was entirely my own fault. I had been in the mountain region on
several occasions and had never felt any inconvenience from
the altitude; in fact thought myself immune. Helena is four
thousand feet above sea level, not a very serious matter. But
Mount Helena rises twelve hundred feet higher. After taking dinner with a friend and his wife on a Sunday afternoon,
Mount Helena looked inviting to me and I climbed up the
face of it, which is quite steep, to the very summit, where

I had a splendid view of the city and broad valley. I had
on several occasions been at higher elevations and had felt
no discomfort. I had spent a couple of weeks in the moun-
tains of Colorado, trout fishing, at an altitude of more than
six thousand feet. But the strenuous climb affected me. I
became dizzy the next morning and staggered about. Mrs.
Haugen joined me at this very time, and naturally was much
alarmed. I called on a physician. He gave me an electric
treatment, which I believe was a mistake. What I needed
was absolute rest, instead of an electric shock. I did not improve within the week, and we left for home, where I soon recovered. When I returned to Helena later I took care not
to over-exert myself physically, and I had no trouble.

My service in Montana continued with interruptions for
about three years, or until a permanent commission had been
established by the legislature in 1923. I took part in drafting the act.

THE CLARK-DALEY CAMPAIGN

I have referred to the fact that Mr. Clark, the copper
king, and later United States senator, as president of the
constitutional convention in 1889, had taken good care of
that prominent industry in the new state. His later election
to the senate became somewhat of a national scandal.

Jerry Murphy, private secretary to Governor La Follette at the beginning of his gubernatorial administration,
resigned from that position and took up newspaper work at
Helena. He now resides in San Diego, California. Murphy
is a clever writer, and while in Helena he produced "The
Comic History of Montana," wherein he dwells at length
on the senatorial campaign to which I refer. The fight was
long and bitter, and every means to secure the votes of members was resorted to. Murphy tells of a member whom neither side had been able to secure for its candidate. One eve-

ning in his room at the hotel a wad of paper was flung in
over the transom. On opening it it was found to contain
many thousand dollars in money. No writing accompanied
it to indicate the sender. He took the package to the House
the next morning, placed it on the speaker's table and told
his story. The money was deposited in the state treasury,
and has never been claimed.

During the session in the winter of 1923 one of the members of the legislature from Silver Bow County was a former
district judge (corresponding to our circuit judges), a Mr.
Denny, a very clever and witty old fellow. In the hotel lobby
one evening the subject of legislators' salaries came up. The
members in Montana are paid ten dollars a day, the session
beginning, under the constitution, on January first and end-
ing March first. There was the same general complaint of
inadequacy of compensation that we hear in Wisconsin.
Judge Denny remarked that a man could not stay in Helena and pay his legitimate expenses and come out whole,
and added, "and there is not a transom in this whole ——
hotel." The allusion seemed well understood. Denny was
from Butte, Clark's former home.

Clark resided in New York, but retained his large interests in the copper mines of Montana, and the legislature
began to study how his estate could be reached by way of
an inheritance tax, an act of that character having been
passed in 1919 or 1921. It was necessarily in general terms,
and was a graduated tax. But, lo and behold! When it
came to be administered it was discovered that the steps of
gradation were carried on up to $25,000 of taxable estate,
but there was no provision for any tax on amounts in excess
of that figure. The bill had been thus amended while in conference between the two houses; no one seemed to know by
whom. The supreme court found the language so plain that
it was not open to construction. But Clark was still alive,
and in the session of 1923 I assisted in drafting a bill, largely

on the Wisconsin model, and that became the law. Upon Clark's death a few years later his estate paid a very large inheritance tax—undoubtedly the largest thus far paid in Montana. I do not know what the final assessment was, but the member of the commission who made the estimates wrote me during the pendency of the proceedings that it might exceed one and a half million dollars. So Montana caught up with Clark at last, but only after he had retired to his last rest. It was generally suspected that the Clark interests had managed to mutilate the former act to protect his interest even after his death.

Closely bound up with the copper interests was the Montana Power Company, which furnished power to the mines and also to the smelting works at Great Falls, as well as to the several hundred miles of the Chicago, Milwaukee and St. Paul Railroad operated by electricity through the mountain region of that and adjoining states. It is one of the largest hydro-electric power plants in the country. This large property had been assessed by the state board for years at between thirty-seven and thirty-eight million dollars. After giving the matter considerable study and applying the rules generally adopted in Wisconsin, I fixed the valuation at about fifty-three million dollars, and notified the company. Their representative immediately appeared. He admitted my figure as being warranted, "If other property was assessed at its true value." To this I agreed. There seemed never to have been any earnest effort in the state at an equitable equalization. After the organization of the new tax commission that body increased my valuation, and the matter was contested in the courts. I attended the hearing in court at Butte. Due largely to the absence of equalization between this and other large properties the matter was finally compromised at, I believe, something like forty-eight million dollars in valuation of this single property. The general manager and the secretary of the power company were al-

ways friendy and courteous to me personally. I always met
them openly, as had been our method in Wisconsin, a plan
which seemed not to have been the habit of their assessment
authorities.

The Pullman Company had for years paid no tax in
Montana. After consulting the governor it was thought
best to impose a license fee. The railroad valuation is distributed to the local governmental units, and it seemed desirable to secure this revenue to the state treasury. A license
fee of $100,000 was imposed. I drafted the bill.

The members of the legislature were alert and wide-
awake. I enjoyed the two months with them. The committee on taxation treated me with the utmost consideration
and confidence. I felt that they were earnest in their effort
to give the people the very best service. A lady member, Mrs.
Facey, was given charge of the inheritance bill and conducted
it to a successful passage. A member from Butte, also a
member of the committee, and an attorney, objected to the
bill. The term "intangibles" was used in the draft. He said
he had never seen that word before and did not know its
meaning. The assessment laws are very minute as to classi-
fications of property, and upon examining local assessment
rolls it was found that the assessors designated even libraries
by classes, such as law libraries, medical libraries, etc. It was
found that no law library (at any rate by that designation)
had been assessed in Silver Bow County. The attorney
had jeered some at the term, saying that it must be a Wisconsin word, having reference to my authorship. I suggested to Mrs. Facey that if he tried to spring that question
on the floor she might retort that she was not surprised at
his ignorance as there was not a single law book in his county,
and she could prove it by the assessment roll.

A sixty-day session is too short, I concluded, noticing
the congested condition of the calendar at the close.

Governor Dixon had recommended and advocated a license fee on minerals, and a bill passed the House, but failed in the Senate. An initiative bill, under their constitution, with that purpose in view, was ratified by popular vote in the following election. A strange inconsistency appeared. Governor Dixon made his campaign for reëlection largely on that issue. The voters endorsed his bill, but elected his opponent. The result was undoubtedly brought about by bitter personal war against the candidate, when the measure he advocated was so entirely fair.

I have the greatest respect for Governor Dixon, and was glad to learn from the press a few days ago that he has been appointed first assistant to the Secretary of the Interior, thus becoming closely allied with the Hoover administration, where he will render admirable service. Throughout he has been a consistent Progressive in the best sense of the term, and never apologized for his activity as manager of the Roosevelt campaign in 1912.

The state treasurer was a firm supporter of the governor as a fellow member of the Board of Equalization. He was J. W. Walker of Kalispell. Mr. Walker was a former resident of Oshkosh, Wisconsin, where he spent his boyhood days and early manhood. He was educated at the Oshkosh Normal School. The governor appointed him head of the newly created tax commission. The title, however, of State Board of Equalization was retained, in order to comply with the language of the constitution.

DICK THE COUNTY SPLITTER

In 1923 the legislature of Montana consisted of one hundred members of the house of representatives and fifty-four senators. Somewhat on the model of the federal government, each county is given one senator. Many of the counties are quite large, the state being the third in area, exceeded

only by Texas and California. A county can be divided upon petition by taxpayers, or possibly voters, asking for the
creation of a new county and designating its proposed county
seat. This has undoubtedly led to some abuse. An individual, whom we will call "Dick," had made it his business
to assist any local community aspiring to become a county
seat. He would engage for a consideration to secure the
necessary number of petitioners. Local real estate owners
and business men of the proposed new center quite naturally
fell for this prospect of building up a new center. The new
county seat must not be within a certain distance of the old
one. There was plenty of leeway as a rule. The promoter
of this novel enterprise became known as "Dick, the County
Splitter."

In the summer of 1923 the State Bar Association of
Montana met at Hunter's Hot Springs near Livingston.
I was asked to address the meeting. This I did, dwelling
at some length on the methods pursued in Wisconsin. I
also suggested wherein I thought their state board had failed
to comply with the provisions of their constitution. For instance, the constitution provides that after determining the
valuation of a railroad in the state the board shall distribute
such valuation to the counties and smaller governmental
units "in proportion to the miles of railway laid" in each.
This had never been complied with. The length of the line
had been used instead of the length of track. I believe
my talk had the approval of the bar. There was the necessary dinner and accompanying speeches. Some witticisms
were indulged in, but they all seemed to center on the Vol-
stead law.

CHAPTER VIII

Concluding Observations

My public service may be said to have terminated with the attendance on the Montana Board of Assessment during the legislative session of 1923. Commencing with the appointment as court reporter in the spring of 1874 it had, with short interruptions, continued for nearly fifty years. I had had my share; and had enjoyed the associations and friendships formed. Good and loyal support when a candidate for elective office, I had enjoyed. I have not endeavored to name the many loyal supporters, as such effort would be useless, as memory becomes more treacherous with age, and would result in seeming unfair discrimination. I bear them all in kindly remembrance.

RAILROAD ASSESSMENTS

I have said that I had perhaps more direct charge of railroad valuation than either of my colleagues while a member of the tax commission, due largely to the fact that I personally kept record of sales of stocks and bonds as recorded on the market. While the representatives of the companies, like other taxpayers, consistently appeared and asked for lower valuations, we must have appeared to them as reasonably fair, compared with assessment officials of some of the other states. When I returned from Montana in 1921, the tax commissioners of the Northwestern, of the Omaha, and the Burlington came to me, separately, and asked me to com-

pute according to our Wisconsin methods the valuation of
their respective properties in Iowa, in South Dakota, and in
Nebraska.   In each case they said, "We do not ask you to
depart from the method you have followed in Wisconsin."

Litigation was pending in the federal courts, involving
these assessments. I readily complied, attended hearings in
Chicago before a magistrate in chancery, also made several
trips to Omaha where cases were pending in the federal
court. I have felt that this was what might be termed a
"semi-public" duty, although performed more directly at
the request of the taxpayer and at his expense. I made care-
ful computations and appeared as a witness. In these states,
as in Montana, the board consists of elective state officials,
whose first duties are devoted to their respective administrative offices, and assessments of public utilities become necessarily a secondary matter.

I think it may be truthfully said that the Wisconsin tax
commission had the respect of the tax officials of the railroads. We discussed our methods with them openly, and
showed them how the values were obtained. A member of
the Montana board hesitated at this. I suggested that as the
board had the last word, there was nothing to be alarmed at,
and if any injustice were pointed out, it might be corrected
on the spot.

Mr. Crandon was for many years the representative of
the Northwestern Railway,—the dean of the railway men
regularly appearing before us. He was a scholarly gentleman, accurate and precise in his language,—never using
"minimize," when he meant "minify," evidently recognizing
the impossibility of minimizing inequalities in assessments,
while they may be and should be minified. His name is per-
petuated in the county seat of Forest County. He was a re-
gent of Northwestern University. His successor was T. A.

Polleys, who had served in the same capacity for the Omaha and came to the Northwestern because of the practical union of those companies. A former resident of Madison, an indefatigable worker was Polleys; scrutinizing carefully all the figures submitted by the commission, not only those on railroads, but those upon which we based the real estate valuations of the state, which made the basis of the tax rate applied to railroads. These men have both passed away.

John A. Murphy, one of the general counsel of the Great Northern was an old friend and acquaintance from Pierce County, where he was born and spent his boyhood. In fact he began his study of law in the office of Smith and Haugen, in River Falls. He served one term in the assembly from Pierce County. He soon left us, however, for a wider field, and has prospered. In a material way, he has undoubtedly been a gainer by leaving behind him the political ambitions he at one time seemed to cherish.

LITERARY ATTAINMENTS

I hesitate to use the word "attainments," for I cannot claim that I possess them. I loved to read from childhood; in school and college I managed to maintain good standings in my classes. But my years in college were necessarily cut short. I have, however, kept up my reading habits. Professor Larson, President of Luther College, was in Madison one day in the early eighties, while I was railroad commissioner, and took dinner with us. He asked me at the table if I kept up my language studies. I answered that I kept up my German fairly well; that I read the *Germania* regularly, and some German books; that I got a little Latin through law books. But I expressed regret that I had not had the opportunity to get any knowledge of French. To this he replied:

"Do not speak to me of opportunity. I know you. Get a French book and a dictionary, and 'go at it.'" He was too precise in his English to use the slang phrase "go at it," but we were talking in Norwegian, and it meant that. The result was that I bought a French dictionary and Voltaire's *History of Charles XII* the very next day, and have read French for my own entertainment and I hope with some mental profit, ever since. One of the most interesting histories I have read is Michelet's *History of France,* which I read after moving to Madison. In Washington I took a few lessons in what was supposed to be conversational French; but I cannot claim to have profited to any degree by that experience. The only other member of the House of Representatives who indulged in a similar luxury, as far as I knew, was big Tom Reed. We did not exchange thoughts in French, however.

During one of my political campaigns I met at Superior the editor of a French paper published in St. Paul—I think it was *L'Etoile du Nord,* or *The North Star.* He started to read some political item from this paper, but his English failed him. I asked to see it, and translated it easily to his great surprise. It is naturally more difficult to translate into a language with which you are less familiar than from it into your own. That is helping me in French. History is probably the easiest to pick up in that respect. But I have read all of Balzac's novels as well, and reread many of them. While in Washington I became well acquainted with Mr. Spofford, librarian of the Congressional Library, and he frequently suggested reading matter to me. When long debates were on in the House in Washington it was quite common for members not immediately interested in the matter under discussion to occupy their time in writing at their desks, or reading. Ex-Governor Gear of Iowa, was one of such members, and knew of my habits in that respect. He came to my seat one day, and said, "Haugen, what are you reading now?"

I said, "Listen to this, and see if you recognize it."

I read a few lines running something like this:

> Came the ancient Agamoninan,
> Sat himself upon the cross-tree, etc.

"Why," he said, "that's from Hiawatha."

I said, "No, it is not from Hiawatha, but it is where Longfellow got some of his ideas and the meter. It is 'Kalevala' the epic poem of Finland."

He was surprised; said he wanted the book when I had finished it. Later he told me that it was a new discovery to him; that he and Mrs. Gear had enjoyed it very much.

Longfellow was familiar with the literature of northern Europe as his *Tales of a Wayside Inn* bears witness.

I have among my books a novel, *The Surgeon's Stories,* written in Swedish by Zakarias Topelius, a Finlander, one of the most interesting historical novels, in my opinion, ever published, covering a period of more than one hundred and fifty years, beginning with the Thirty Years' War about the time of the death of Gustavus Adolphus. It is an exposition of the habits and customs not only of Sweden and Finland, but of northern and middle Europe at that time.

A PIONEER AGAIN

The *River Falls Journal* last July published among its "Fifty Years Ago" items the following, as of July 3, 1879:

> N. P. Haugen now uses a machine called a typewriter for transcribing his shorthand court reports.

It was a "typewriter" to the editor, and no doubt the first in Pierce County. About that time machines began to be used by some attorneys; but generally they used capitals entirely. Mine had the double set of types.

Among the characters at the bar during my reportorial days I may mention a few, though belated and somewhat out of chronological order. Alexander Meggett of the firm of Meggett and Teall, of Eau Claire, leading attorneys of that city, prided himself on his oratorical ability. He closed his argument to the jury on one occasion at Alma with somewhat of a flourish, and before taking his seat turned to me saying *sotto voce,* "Did you get my peroration?" Unfortunately I was not reporting the arguments of counsel, and Meggett's peroration was forever lost.

Mr. Cousins, father of the president of the State Historical Society, had a certain humorous quaintness that sometimes surprised the bar. He once objected to a question asked the witness, and the court asked him to make his objection more specific. Mr. Cousins replied "that the question is incompetent, irrelevant, immaterial, impertinent and impudent."

Nelson Wheeler, senior partner of the firm of Wheeler and Marshall, of Chippewa Falls, never passed by a joke without regard to court or jury. In those days candidates for admission to the bar were examined in open court, by a committee appointed by the court. Wheeler being one of the older practitioners was usually one of the committee. He had two standard questions which he never failed to put to the candidate:

"How would you endorse a verbal order?"

"Do you think a man can be convicted of highway robbery, if the highway is not legally laid out?"

A story of an examination in Pierce County,—before my day as reporter—ran as follows. Spence White, father of F. M. White, at present a member of the Board of Law

Examiners, was a strict adherent to rules of the old order, technical, and never failed to demur if opportunity offered. He also looked after his fees with vigilance. John Dale was an old resident of the country, living on a small farm in the Trimbelle Valley, where he also ran a small sawmill. Dale had been justice of the peace in his town for years, and had practiced before other justices. He made up his mind that he wished to be admitted to the bar, and appeared at the term of the Circuit Court. Mr. White quite naturally was on the examining committee. It seems that shortly before this event Mr. White had brought an action of replevin for a span of mules, and as his client seemed to him of questionable financial standing, he had taken a chattel mortgage on the mules to secure his fee. During the examination White straightened up to his best, and said, "Mr. Dale, how would you commence an action of replevin?"

The answer was as prompt as unexpected, "I would take a chattel mortgage on the mules."

He was promptly admitted as a brother in the profession; but there is no record of his practice as an attorney. He was a clever old fellow, one to be reckoned with in county politics.

E. H. Ives was an early attorney of Pierce County and served one term in the State Senate. In those early days, if a person wished to have his name changed, he must apply to the legislature. Such an application was before the Senate on behalf of some Norwegian. Objection was made that there was too much time taken up by such private bills. But Ives interposed with the remark, "The Good Book says that the leopard cannot change his spots nor the Ethiopian his skin, but it nowhere says that a Norwegian cannot change his name." The bill passed.

A REPUBLICAN

I do not boast that I always vote the ticket straight, but with a single exception I have voted for the Republican candidate for president. In 1872 I failed to vote as I was absent at the time as a student at Ann Arbor. I would have voted for Grant. Think I may claim to have been one of the very first Hoover men in Wisconsin. The *Literary Digest* in the early part of 1920 asked its subscribers to submit their first and second choice for president. I submitted my first choice as Hoover, and my second as Coolidge. Have never regretted these selections; have had them both, but in reverse order.

I have seen many changes in the domestic, industrial, and political life of Wisconsin. In August 1928 I attended a picnic, or home-coming, in my old town of Martell. The gathering met on the banks of Rush River on the premises of William Kay, son of one of three pioneer Frenchmen of the valley. The old settlers of my boyhood had disappeared. One veteran of the Civil War, Mr. Babcock, showed up alone. Some forty or fifty men and women of middle age and younger hailed me as "Uncle." They necessarily represented several later generations.

Not a single horse appeared on the scene; all automobiles—here, where in my youth people were proud when they could drive to church on a Sunday with a yoke of oxen, and some years later with horses before a lumber wagon! I have certainly lived through and witnessed strange and important developments, all undoubtedly tending to lighten labor and make life more comfortable. If I have any curiosity as to the future, it would be to witness the changes of the next half century. But with old age necessarily comes physical decay, and I would consider that price too high. I have had my share of early hardships, which I enjoyed at the time; I have enjoyed my later labors, and I hope I have been of some service to my fellowmen.

A little family history may not be amiss before closing. In 1856 a family moved into the little burg of Martell, Ole Rasmusson with his wife and one child, baptized as Ingeborg, a good old Norwegian name, but generally known as Belle. Mr. Rasmusson was a cabinet maker from the old country; but there was little demand for his craft in Martell, where a bedstead was easily provided by nailing a few boards to four posts obtained from waste at the sawmill, or secured by cutting four round posts in the surrounding timber. So Mr. Rasmusson became a merchant, the first one, I think, in the village. His stock consisted of a few family supplies, like coffee, always a Norwegian necessity, sugar, and other household requirements. Mrs. Rasmusson was a woman of some education, bringing some knowledge of English and German from her native country. But she adapted herself readily to her surroundings. When Belle was old enough to attend school she dressed her, as I thought, so much like a little doll, that I in my buckskin hardly dared look at her. But some nineteen years later I was more courageous, and after due approaches, secured her affirmative answer and our compact was duly confirmed March 1, 1875. We have lived a happy life and have enjoyed good health quite universally. One daughter, Constance, has been a blessing to us. She is now Mrs. Herman Legreid of Wauwatosa, and is the happy mother of two daughters just entering their teens, Christine and Constance, the delight of grandparents as well as parents. Our daughter and her husband are both graduates of our State University. Mr. Rasmusson died in 1887. My mother-in-law spent most of her later years with us in River Falls, and remained as sweet and dear a

mother-in-law as she had been a wife and mother. She died
in 1901 while visiting another daughter in Chicago.

Looking over the past and present I can say:

> Time rolls his ceaseless course. The race of yore
>   Who danced our infancy upon their knee,
> And told our marvelling boyhood legends store
>   Of their strange ventures happed by land or sea,
> How are they blotted from the things that be!
>   How few, all weak, and withered of their force,
> Wait on the verge of dark eternity,
>   Like stranded wrecks, the tide returning hoarse,
> To sweep them from our sight! Time rolls his cease-
>   less course.